C000318829

indian
FLAVOURS

MARUT SIKKA

indian FLAVOURS

Photographs
DHEERAJ PAUL

Lustre Press
·
Roli Books

All rights reserved. No part of this publication
may be transmitted or reproduced in any
form or by any means without prior
permission from the publisher.

ISBN: 81-7436-326-2

© Roli & Janssen BV 2005
Second impression 2006
Published in India by Roli Books
in arrangement with
Roli & Janssen BV The Netherlands
M-75 Greater Kailash II Market
New Delhi 110 048, India
Ph: ++91-11-29212782, 29210886.
Fax: ++91-11-29217185.
E-mail: roli@vsnl.com
Website: rolibooks.com

Editor: Neeta Datta
Design: Arati Subramanyam
Layout: Naresh Mondal
Production: Naresh Nigam

Printed and bound in Singapore

contents

Dedication

For my wife, Anusuiya, the real driving force behind me, without whose unwavering love and support, this book would not have been possible.

Acknowledgements

I wish to thank Chef Mohammed Ilyas, Santha Kumari Amma, and Manish Bafila for all their assistance in researching, creating and writing these recipes. And Neeta Datta, editor Roli Books, for her exemplary patience in bearing with my erratic schedule and making this book a reality. Above all Mr Jiggs Kalra, my teacher, who opened the world of food to me.

*i*n India food is *naivaidya*. It is sacred. And those who prepare it must enter the kitchen in a state of purity. Food here is also *kala* or an art and those who savour it must be able to immerse themselves in its *rasa*, or essence. While in some communities it is a discipline meant to cleanse the soul in others it is an indulgence meant for the celebration of the senses. A potpourri not just of sight, sound and taste, cuisine in India is also an amalgam of social, cultural, and economic exchanges down the ages.

While historically indigenous ingredients abound in this land of milk and honey (the Greek Megasthenes was amazed to see Indians 'drink honey out of

introduction

giant bamboo canes') what has helped Indian cuisine evolve is the constant integration of foreign influences. From the end of the first century BC, long-distance trade has played a major role in the cultural, religious, and artistic interactions that took place between the major centres of civilization in Europe and Asia. The trade routes later referred to as the Silk and Spice Routes, principally were used to transfer raw materials, foodstuff, and luxury goods. Over the years, the Greeks, Chinese, Arabs, Mongols, Afghans, Portuguese, Dutch, French and even the British have disclosed their culinary prowess to the Indians and like an amorphous giant we have absorbed all their secrets. It was this confluence of style with the array of available spices that has encouraged experimentation and a keen adaptation of numerous influences.

To recognize the greatness of Indian cuisine one must pay homage to its regional cadences. Even the humble mustard can illustrate these variations. The pungency of mustard seeds can colour the relationship of a Bengali bride with her mother-in-law for it is a measure of her skill to be able to grind it without mishap. And yet in the North it is the shoot and the leaves that seem to leave grown Punjabi men begging for more. Entire festivals are hinged around its growth and it is often used as a seasonal barometer.

The *kalpa-vriksh* or the wish-fulfilling tree is an integral part of all coastal food. This is the coconut tree. Every home in the South of India would boast of at least a couple of these trees. The coconut fruit, its milk and its oil is as much a necessary ingredient in the southern kitchen as is salt. Yet there are very few northern taste buds that would be able to palate such a liberal dose of coconut.

Apart from variety, spices in India are also invaluable for their versatility. Food is often ingested for its therapeutic values. Turmeric is at once antiseptic and anti-inflammatory. It is the aspirin of the spice world. It is also auspicious. On the day of the marriage a bride is traditionally bathed after an *ubtan* (soothing paste) of turmeric and sandalwood has been applied to her. And so the ordinary spice straddles medicinal, aromatic and beauty therapy with élan.

Cuisine in India is also seasonal. Often this is necessary as the cyclical variations in climate are extreme (like in the North) and the natural availability of particular herbs, vegetables, and fruits are severely effected. But the division sometimes need not be so obvious. It is not just availability that determines a category like *garmi* (heat) or *sardi* (coolness) but a subtle calculation of its inherent *guna* (value) and its resultant *taseer* (effect). In fact, the Chinese concept of the yin and yang of food is said to be an offshoot of this Indian theory.

Mercifully in spite of all the scientific speculation that seems to accompany every herb and spice—what gives Indian cuisine its flavour and texture is its sensuousness. Perhaps no other cuisine in the world has to deal with as much visual and aromatic opulence. And the drama of Indian cuisine could never be accomplished without a certain abandon. While it is not enough to be a slave to the spices it is not even enough to be its mistress. Every dish varies from home to home and in that lies its innate Indianness.

Sreya Seth

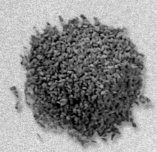

Carom or Bishop's weed (ajwain): is native to India, but cultivated in many parts of the world today. Sometimes chewed raw for its medicinal value, carom is more often used to add that extra punch to breads and starchy foods. It has properties that aid digestion, and is also used to relieve asthma and arthritis. It is believed to contain male aphrodisiac properties.

Substitutes: Dried thyme

Asafoetida (hing): though not native to India, it is used extensively as a substitute to the forbidden onion and garlic by the Brahmin, trader and Jain castes in India. Uncooked asafoetida has an offensive odour, hence it is used in very small quantities. It prevents flatulence and indigenous medicine advocates it as a cure for respiratory ailments. It is said to improve a singer's voice, if eaten raw.

Substitutes: A mixture of garlic and onion powder

Dry mango powder (amchur): is sun-dried raw mango slices ground into a fine powder. Primarily used by the affluent class in ancient India as a souring agent for curries and stir-fries, it is also used for adding tang to pickles and chutneys. The powder is astringent, high in vitamin C, and is used to prevent scurvy. It is an essential ingredient in a variety of Indian digestives called chooran.

Substitutes: Lemon juice or tamarind

Green cardamom (choti elaichi): is almost certainly among the world's oldest spices (about 4000 years old) with historical references to it. It is used as a top-note flavouring for many Indian savory and sweet dishes. It is said to have aphrodisiac qualities and was used to counter obesity. Cardamom was offered to the Gods in ancient India and is also used to a large extent as a mouth freshener, though the uninitiated may find the raw taste overbearing.

Cloves (laung): native to Indonesia, this overpowering spice resembles unopened flower buds and is used largely in India as an integral part of the Indian all-purpose spice garam masala. It is also used with charcoal embers and ghee to smoke certain kebabs, dishes and drinks. Whole clove has been used as a household remedy for toothaches due to its anaesthetic properties.

Coriander seeds (dhaniya): is most likely native to the Middle East, but has been in use in India for thousands of years. This seed with an unique flavour, is the mainstay of curries across the world, providing the basal notes and is often used in a larger quantity than the other spices. Freshly roasted and coarsely pounded seeds are also used. Oil derived from the seed is a strong antibiotic, used extensively in medieval times. It also cures minor stomach ailments, specially flatulence and colic.

Green coriander (hara dhaniya): often referred to as cilantro, the leaves of the coriander plant are almost certainly the second most (after cumin) used herb in Indian cooking. They have a distinctive aromatic smell and are added to Indian curries for their flavour or used as a garnish. The leaf paste is used to make many kinds of fresh chutneys and dips. The herb stimulates appetite and aids in digestion. It is also said to be an aphrodisiac.

Curry leaf (kari patta): the mainstay of most southern Indian dishes—non vegetarian or otherwise. These small leaves have mildly pungent scent which is very delicate and can dissipate if not used with caution. Curry leaves cure stomach upsets and are sometimes used to prevent nausea.

Fennel seeds (moti saunf): an import from the Mediterranean, the seeds are used more in India, though all parts of the plant are highly aromatic and edible. Fennel is an intrinsic part of mouth fresheners in India, and is occasionally used in cooking. It was used in medieval India as a remedy for snake bites and the water in which fennel seeds is soaked overnight is an excellent eye lotion.

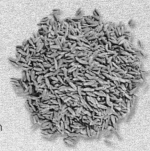

Cumin (jeera): is often confused with caraway (shahi jeera), resembling the latter in appearance. Cumin is the mainstay of most Indian curries, dishes, rice, and aperitifs. Along with coriander it forms the base of most curry powders. It is a great remedy for flatulence and other stomach ailments. Roasted cumin seed powder is at the core of the Indian digestive chooran.

Garlic (lasan): has been the horror of sorcerers, werewolves, warlocks and vampires in folklore for millennia. Native to harsh Siberia, communities in India either love it for its taste or abhor it for its ability to arouse frenzied passions. Garlic is an antiseptic, antibiotic and antifungal, a fact advocated by modern medicine. A daily dose of 8-10 raw garlic cloves is recommended for good health.

Mace (javitri): is the bright crimson cover of the nutmeg seed shell. It is a powerful spice and is used sparingly in Indian cuisine. Almost never used whole, it is more commonly used as mace powder, which is often paired with green cardamom to give top notes to mostly curries.

Mint (pudina): for centuries has been associated with hospitality and wisdom. In India, fresh leaves are frequently blended with spices to make a chutney. It is a perfect accompaniment to most kebabs and snacks. Chopped mint is occasionally added to Indian savouries to enhance flavour. It aids digestion, hiccups and is used for throat and sinus ailments. Concentrated mint leaf extract with sugar is prescribed to prevent nausea as a household remedy.

Mustard seeds (rai): form the perfect marriage with curry leaves and cooking without them is inconceivable for most south Indians. The east Indians love the paste that is derived by grinding the seeds. Freshly ground mustard is often prescribed for stings and bites. In India, warm mustard oil is often used as a massage medium for stiff necks, rheumatism, and hair.

Nigella or Onion seeds (kalonji): resemble small black sesame seeds and have a mildly bitter taste. Roasted seeds give out maximum flavour hence are sprinkled over India's popular bread—the naan. The seeds are also intrinsic to a special five-spice mixture used predominantly in east India—*panch phoron.* Nigella is used in Indian medicine against indigestion and bowel complaints. It is also used to induce labour and promote lactation.

Lamb Stock
Yields: 5 cups

Take 450 gm / 1 lb lamb bones, 1 medium-sized onion, peeled and pierced with 1 whole clove, 1 carrot (*gajar*), peeled, 1/2 cup green coriander (*hara dhaniya*), 12 garlic (*lasan*) cloves, peeled, 1 tsp salt, 8 black peppercorns (*sabut kaali mirch*), and 1" piece ginger, roughly chopped.

In a stock pot, combine the lamb bones with about 12 cups of water, or enough to cover. Bring the mixture to the boil and skim off the froth. Add the remaining ingredients and simmer on low heat, partially covered, for 2 hours. Strain the broth through a fine strainer, discarding the bones and vegetables. Allow the stock to cool. Chill in the refrigerator and skim off the fat. The stock can be frozen for up to 2 months.

Chicken Stock
Yields: 6 cups

Take 2 1/4 kg / 5 lb chicken bones, 1 large onion, peeled, quartered, 1 large carrot (*gajar*), roughly chopped, 1/2 cup green coriander (*hara dhaniya*), roughly chopped, 2 large leeks, cut in half lengthwise and washed, 2 bay leaves (*tej patta*), 1 cinnamon, 2" stick, and 12 black peppercorns (*sabut kaali mirch*).

Place all the ingredients in a large stock pot and cover with water. Bring the mixture to the boil on high heat and skim off the froth. Reduce heat and simmer for 3-4 hours, continuing to skim impurities from time to time while the stock cooks. Remove from heat and let the stock sit for 10-15 minutes, then strain through a fine strainer. Allow the stock to cool. Chill in the refrigerator and skim off the fat. The stock can keep for about 1 week in the refrigerator.

Vegetable Stock
Yields: 8 cups

Take 5 celery stalks, sliced, 4 large carrots, sliced, 2 large onions, sliced, 1/2 head of green cabbage, sliced, 1 small bunch of green coriander (*hara dhaniya*, 1 head of garlic, cut in half crosswise to expose the cloves, 12 black peppercorns (*sabut kaali mirch*), 3 bay leaves (*tej patta*), and 1" piece ginger (*adrak*), roughly chopped.

In a stock pot, combine all the ingredients and cover with cold water. Bring the mixture to the boil on high heat and skim off the froth with a ladle. Reduce heat and simmer gently for 45-60 minutes. Strain through a fine strainer, cool and refrigerate. The stock can keep for up to 4-5 days in the refrigerator.

Mint Chutney

Take 1 cup mint (*pudina*) leaves, chopped, 1 1/2 cups green coriander (*hara dhaniya*), chopped, 1 tsp cumin (*jeera*) seeds, 6 garlic (*lasan*) cloves, chopped, 2 green chillies, chopped, 1 raw mango, peeled, chopped, juice of 2 lemons (*nimbu*), and salt to taste.

Blend all the ingredients into a smooth paste, using water if required. Refrigerate in an airtight container and use as required.

Coconut Milk

Grate the coconut and press through a muslin cloth to obtain the first (thick) extract. Blend the grated coconut with equal quantity of water and strain similarly to obtain the second (thin) extract. Mix the extracts to make the coconut milk as mentioned in the recipes.

If refrigerated, this can stay for up to 3-4 days.

Cinnamon: Dalchini

Strongly aromatic, sweet, pleasant and warm

Cumin Seeds: Jeera

Strongly aromatic; the aroma is characteristic and is modified by frying or dry roasting

Asafoetida: Hing

Very strong smell, rather repugnant, remotely similar to (not altogether fresh) garlic

Black Peppercorns: Kaali Mirch

Pungent and aromatic, which is strongest in white pepper and weakest in green pepper while black and green are more aromatic than the white one

Dry Mango Powder: Amchur

Sour, with a slight resinous overtone

Mace: Javitri

Strongly aromatic,
resinous and warm
in taste

Cardamom: Elaichi

Black cardamom is fresh and
aromatic with a strong smoky
flavour, while green cardamom is
sweet, aromatic and pleasant

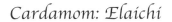

Cloves: Laung

Strongly aromatic, intensive
fragrance, fiery with a
burning taste

Coriander Seeds: Dhaniya

Pleasant aroma
with warm, nutty and
spicy qualities

Fennel Seeds: Saunf

Sweet and very
aromatic

the spice family

Roasted Raw Mango Cooler

Aam ka Panna

Mangoes (*aam*), raw	6	Cumin (*jeera*) seeds, roasted	1 tsp
Sugar, dissolved in 1 cup of water		Mint (*pudina*) leaves, blended	
to make syrup	¼ cup	to a fine paste	1 tbsp
Black rock salt (*kaala namak*)	1 tsp	Salt to taste	

Method

Roast the mangoes in a baking tray for 45 minutes at 180°C / 350°F.

Remove the pulp from the mangoes and discard the skin and the seeds.

Blend the pulp to a fine paste with the sugar syrup. Add 3 cups of iced water and blend well.

Add the remaining ingredients and blend further. Remove, adjust the seasoning and serve in tall glasses.

Spiced Yoghurt Drink

Chaas

Yoghurt (*dahi*), 1-day old	400 gm / 14 oz	Cumin seeds, roasted, powdered	1 tsp
Salt to taste		Black rock salt (*kaala namak*) to taste	
Cumin (*jeera*) seeds	1 tsp	Green coriander (*hara dhaniya*),	
Green chilli, medium-sized,		finely chopped	1 tbsp
deseeded, finely chopped	1	Mint (*pudina*) leaves, finely chopped	1 tbsp
Ginger (*adrak*), 1″ piece, finely chopped	1		

Method

Whisk the yoghurt in a bowl; add 2 cups of iced water and blend well.

Add the remaining ingredients, blend for a minute.

Remove from blender, adjust the seasoning and serve in tall glasses.

Gram Flour Fish Fritters

Amritsari Macchi

Sole with skin, boneless, cut into 3″ fillets	450 gm / 1 lb		Water	¹/₄ cup
			Egg	1
Step I:			**Step II:**	
Gram flour (besan)	5 tbsp		Mustard (sarson) oil for deep-frying	2 cups
Garlic (lasan) paste	3 tbsp		Dry mango powder (amchur)	2 tsp
Ginger (adrak) paste	1 tbsp		Cumin (jeera) powder, roasted	1 tsp
Red chilli powder	1 tbsp		Black pepper (kaali mirch) powder	¹/₂ tsp
Carom (ajwain) seeds	1 tsp		Dry fenugreek leaf	
Asafoetida (hing)	1 tsp		(kasoori methi) powder	¹/₂ tsp
Salt to taste			Black rock salt (kaala namak), optional,	
Lemon (nimbu) juice	2 tbsp		can be replaced with salt	¹/₂ tsp

Method

Wash the fish, shake dry and keep aside. Mix the step I ingredients in a bowl and make a smooth batter.

Add the fish to the batter and mix well, ensuring that all the pieces are well coated. Marinate for 30 minutes.

Heat the mustard oil (step II) in a wok on high heat till it starts smoking. Reduce heat until smoking stops and oil reaches medium temperature. Fry the fish in small batches until light golden brown and fully cooked from the inside. Remove to a strainer to drain excess oil.

Mix the step II spices in a small bowl to make the sprinkler spice.

Arrange the fish on a platter, drizzle the sprinkler and serve.

Stuffed Jalapenos
Bharri Mirch

Jalapeno green chillies	10	Tamarind (*imli*), size of a marble	1
Poppy seeds (*khus khus*), roasted	1 tbsp	Coconut (*nariyal*), desiccated	1 cup
Groundnuts (*moongphalli*),		Salt to taste	
without skin, roasted	1 cup	Cooking oil	2 tbsp

Method

Wash the chillies, slit lengthwise, remove all the seeds and keep aside.

Blend the poppy seeds, groundnuts, tamarind, coconut, and salt with a little water to a smooth paste. Check seasoning. Remove to a bowl.

Stuff this paste in the chillies through the slit.

Heat the oil in a pan on medium heat; sauté the green chillies, turning on their sides, until golden brown.

Remove from heat, transfer on to a platter and serve hot.

Cardamom-flavoured Roasted Lamb

Gosht ki Boti

Lamb leg, boneless,		Cumin (*jeera*) powder, roasted	1 tsp
cut into 2″ cubes	450 gm / 1 lb	Green cardamom (*choti elaichi*)	
Step I:		powder	1 tsp
Garlic (*lasan*) paste	3¹/₄ tsp	Black pepper (*kaali mirch*) powder	¹/₂ tsp
Ginger (*adrak*) paste	2¹/₂ tsp	Clove (*laung*) powder	a pinch
Red chilli powder	2 tsp	Nutmeg (*jaiphal*) powder	a pinch
Yoghurt (*dahi*)	100 gm / 3¹/₂ oz	Lemon (*nimbu*) juice	1 tsp
Salt to taste		Green coriander (*hara dhaniya*),	
Step II:		finely chopped	2¹/₂ tbsp
Ghee	6 tbsp	Mint (*pudina*) leaves, finely chopped	5 tbsp
Onions, thinly sliced	1 cup	Ginger, 1″ piece, cut into thin juliennes	1
Gram flour (*besan*), roasted	1¹/₂ tbsp		

Preparation and Cooking time: 1¹/₂ hrs. Serves: 4

Method

Mix the step I ingredients together and rub onto the lamb. Keep aside for a minimum of 45 minutes to a maximum of 4-6 hours.

Heat the ghee (step II) in a pan on medium heat; add onions and sauté until golden brown. Remove one fifth of the fried onions and keep aside. Add ¹/₂ cup of water and continue to sauté until all the moisture dries up. Add marinated lamb, increase heat to medium-high and stir and roast for a minute.

Reduce heat to medium, and continue to stir and roast until fat appears on the sides. Add 1 cup of water (or lamb stock, see p. 13) and bring to the boil. Cover and simmer on low heat, stirring occasionally, until lamb is fully cooked.

Increase heat to medium and continue to stir and roast until fat starts appearing on the sides. Increase heat to high, sprinkle gram flour and roast for a minute. Add cumin, green cardamom, black pepper, clove, and nutmeg powders. Stir for a minute and add lemon juice, green coriander, and mint leaves. Adjust seasoning and remove.

Transfer to a bowl and serve garnished with the reserved fried onions and ginger.

Nutmeg Potato Roundels
Aloo Jaiphali

Preparation and Cooking time: 45 min. Serves: 4

Potatoes, large, washed well, shaken dry	6	Salt to taste	
Ghee	4 tbsp	Nutmeg (*jaiphal*) powder	1/2 tsp
Cumin (*jeera*) seeds	1 1/2 tsp	Vegetable stock (see p. 13)	1/4 cup
Green chillies, deseeded, finely chopped	2	Lemon (*nimbu*) juice	1 tsp
Ginger (*adrak*), 1" piece, finely chopped	1	Green coriander (*hara dhaniya*),	
Coriander (*dhaniya*) powder	1 tsp	finely chopped	2 tbsp
White pepper (*safed mirch*) powder	1 tsp		

Method

Peel the potatoes and cut into thick roundels. Reserve in cold water.

Heat the ghee in a pan on medium heat; add cumin seeds. When the seeds begin to pop, add green chillies, ginger, and potatoes, stir for a minute.

Add coriander and white pepper powders; mix well. Add salt and nutmeg powder; stir. Add vegetable stock (or water) and stir. Cover and simmer on low heat for 15-20 minutes, stirring gently and occasionally, until potatoes are fully cooked. Add more water, if required.

Add lemon juice; stir gently taking care not to break the potatoes. Add green coriander, stir gently. Check seasoning and remove from heat.

Transfer to a bowl and serve.

Potatoes in Cashew Qorma

Aloo ka Qorma

Potatoes, medium-sized, washed, peeled, halved	8	Onions, thinly sliced	I cup
Cooking oil for frying		Cashew nuts (*kaju*), roasted, blended with water to a fine paste	2 tbsp
Step I:		Salt to taste	
Ginger (*adrak*) paste	I³/₄ tsp	Green cardamom powder	I tsp
Garlic (*lasan*) paste	3¹/₄ tsp	Black pepper (*kaali mirch*) powder	¹/₂ tsp
Red chilli powder	I tsp	Nutmeg (*jaiphal*) powder	a pinch
Coriander (*dhaniya*) powder	4 tsp	Lemon (*nimbu*) juice	I tsp
Yoghurt (*dahi*)	¹/₂ cup	Cream	3 tbsp
Step II:		Green coriander (*hara dhaniya*), finely chopped	5 tbsp
Ghee	6 tbsp		
Green cardamom (*choti elaichi*)	4		

Preparation and Cooking time: 50 min. Serves: 4

Method

Heat the oil in a pan; fry the potatoes on low heat. When they rise to the surface, increase heat to high and fry until potatoes are golden brown. Remove and keep aside.

Mix the step I ingredients in a bowl and keep aside.

Heat the ghee (step II) in a pan on medium heat; add green cardamom and stir until the colour changes. Add onions and stir and roast until golden brown. Add ¹/₂ cup of water and continue to stir until all the moisture dries up and the oil appears on the sides.

Add the step I mixture, stir and roast until the oil appears on the sides. Add the cashew paste and continue to roast until the oil appears on the sides again.

Add potatoes and salt. Add I cup of water, green cardamom, black pepper, and nutmeg powders, cover and simmer on low heat for 4-5 minutes or until the potatoes have soaked the gravy. Remove the cover, add lemon juice and stir for a minute. Add cream, stir and remove from heat.

Transfer to a bowl and serve garnished with green coriander.

Asafoetida-tempered Five Grams

Daal Panchmela

Bengal gram (*chana daal*)	¹/₂ cup	Butter	2 tbsp
Split red gram (*toor daal*)	¹/₂ cup	Lemon (*nimbu*) juice	1 tsp
Husked green gram (*moong daal*)	¹/₂ cup	**Step II:**	
Lentil (*masoor*)	¹/₄ cup	Ghee	3 tbsp
Husked black gram (*urad daal*)	¹/₄ cup	Cumin (*jeera*) seeds	1 tsp
Step I:		Asafoetida (*hing*), dissolved in	
Cooking oil	1 tbsp	1 tbsp water	2 pinches
Turmeric (*haldi*) powder	1 tsp	Coriander (*dhaniya*) seeds,	
Red chilli powder	1 tsp	pounded	1¹/₂ tsp
Salt to taste		Dry red chillies (*sookhi lal mirch*)	4
Ginger (*adrak*), finely chopped	1 tsp	Tomatoes, medium-sized, finely chopped	2

Method

Heat the oil (step I) in a wok on medium heat; add all the daals and stir and roast till light golden in colour. Cool, remove from wok and wash well under running water in a strainer for a few minutes, rubbing with your hands. Drain the excess water and keep aside.

Boil the daal in a pot on high heat with 4 cups of water, turmeric, red chilli powders, salt and ginger. When the mixture starts to boil, reduce heat to medium and remove any scum that comes to the surface. Do not stir the mixture.

Add the butter and boil for 30 minutes or until the daal is fully cooked. Reduce heat to low and stir with a ladle crushing the daal on the sides of the pot until a homogenous mixture is formed. Add lemon juice. Remove from heat and keep aside.

Heat the ghee (step II) in a pan on medium heat; add cumin seeds, asafoetida, and pounded coriander; stir well. Add dry red chillies and stir. Add the tomatoes and roast until fat appears on the sides.

Transfer the daal mixture to the pan, mix well and bring to the boil. Remove from heat. Check seasoning.

Transfer to a bowl and serve.

Gram Flour Fritters in Yoghurt Sauce
Kadhi Pakorhi

Step I:

Gram flour (*besan*)	I cup
Spinach (*paalak*), shredded	150 gm / 5 oz
Soda bi-carbonate	a pinch
Salt to taste	
Coriander (*dhaniya*) seeds, crushed	2 tsp
Cumin (*jeera*) seeds	¹/₂ tsp
Ginger (*adrak*), I" piece, finely chopped	I
Green chillies, deseeded, finely chopped	4
Cooking oil for deep-frying	

Step II:

Yoghurt (*dahi*), I-day old	2 cups
Gram flour	5 tbsp
Salt to taste	
Red chilli powder	I tsp
Turmeric (*haldi*) powder	¹/₂ tsp

Step III:

Ghee	4 tbsp
Cumin seeds	I tsp
Coriander seeds	¹/₂ tsp
Black mustard seeds (*rai*)	¹/₂ tsp
Fenugreek seeds (*methi dana*)	¹/₂ tsp
Asafoetida (*hing*)	a pinch
Dry red chillies (*sookhi lal mirch*)	4
Red chilli powder	¹/₂ tsp

Method

Mix all the step I ingredients (except oil) together. Add about 3 tbsp water and mix well.

Heat the oil in a wok; divide the batter equally into small portions and deep-fry, on medium heat, to make golden brown fritters. Remove with a strainer to drain excess oil.

Whisk the yoghurt (step II) with gram flour, salt, red chilli and turmeric powders. Add 2 cups of water and boil the mixture in a pot on medium heat, stirring continuously. Cover and simmer on low heat, stirring occasionally, until a thin sauce-like consistency is obtained.

Add the fritters and bring to the boil, reduce heat to low and simmer, stirring occasionally, until the consistency of the sauce becomes thick. Remove and adjust seasoning.

Heat the ghee (step III) in a pan; sauté the cumin, coriander, mustard, and fenugreek seeds on medium heat for a minute. Add asafoetida; stir. Add dry red chillies and red chilli powder; stir. Remove from heat and pour the tempering into the finished dish. Check the seasoning and serve with steamed rice.

Stir-fried Spinach & Turnip
Paalak Shalgam

Spinach (*paalak*), washed very
well, shaken dry, chopped — 1 cup
Turnips (*shalgam*), diced into
1″ pieces — 500 gm / 1.1 lb
Mustard (*sarson*) oil — 6 tbsp
Cumin (*jeera*) seeds — 1 1/2 tsp
Black cardamom (*badi elaichi*), whole — 4
Garlic (*lasan*) cloves, finely chopped — 16
Onion, medium-sized, finely chopped — 1
Green chillies, deseeded, finely chopped — 2

Ginger (*adrak*), 1″ piece, finely chopped — 1
Vegetable stock (see p. 13) — 1/4 cup
Salt to taste
Red chilli powder — 1 1/2 tsp
Turmeric (*haldi*) powder — 2 tsp
Tomato purée — 3 tbsp
Lemon (*nimbu*) juice — 1 tbsp
Cream — 1/4 cup
Ginger, 1″ piece, cut into juliennes — 1

Preparation and Cooking time: 1 hr. 15 min. Serves: 4

Method

Heat the mustard oil in a pan on high heat till it starts smoking. Reduce heat until smoking stops and oil reaches medium temperature. Add cumin seeds and black cardamom; stir for 2-3 seconds. Add garlic and sauté until golden brown.

Add onion and sauté until light golden brown. Add green chillies and ginger; sauté for a minute. Add turnips, stir. Add vegetable stock (or water), spinach, and salt; stir. Mix in red chilli and turmeric powders. Cover and simmer on low heat for 6-7 minutes.

Remove cover, increase heat to medium and stir and roast until fat appears on the sides. Add tomato purée and stir and roast until fat appears on the sides. Add lemon juice and cream, stir. Check seasoning and remove from heat.

Transfer to a bowl and serve garnished with ginger.

Okra Flavoured with Black Pepper

Bhindi Kaali Mirch

Okra (*bhindi*), small, washed, edges trimmed	225 gm / ½ lb
Cooking oil	4 tbsp
Cumin (*jeera*) seeds	1 tsp
Onion, medium-sized, finely chopped	1
Coriander (*dhaniya*) powder	1 tsp
Turmeric (*haldi*) powder	½ tsp
Ginger (*adrak*), finely chopped	1 tsp
Green chillies, medium-sized, finely chopped	3
Tomato purée	½ cup
Salt to taste	
Black peppercorns (*sabut kaali mirch*), freshly ground	¼ tbsp
Dry mango powder (*amchur*)	1 tsp
Dry fenugreek leaf (*kasoori methi*) powder	1 tsp
Clove (*laung*) powder	a pinch
Ginger, 1″ piece, cut into fine juliennes	1

Method

Boil 2 cups of water in a pot with 1 tsp oil and salt. Add the okra and boil for 5-6 seconds. Remove from heat and strain the okra immediately through a soup strainer. Keep aside.

Heat the oil in a wok on high heat; add cumin seeds. When the seeds begin to pop add onion; reduce heat to medium, stir and roast until the onion turns glossy and translucent. Add the coriander and turmeric powders, ginger and green chillies. Stir for 30 seconds and then add tomato purée; continue to stir and roast until fat appears on the sides.

Add the okra, stir. Add salt, black pepper, mango, fenugreek, and clove powders; stir again. Increase heat to high and continue to stir and roast until okra is cooked. Check seasoning.

Transfer to a bowl and serve garnished with ginger.

Stuffed Bottle Gourd in Cashew Gravy

Bharwaan Lauki

Bottle gourd (*lauki*), 8" long	2	Clove (*laung*) powder	1/2 tsp	
Step I:		Black peppercorns (*sabut kaali mirch*),		
Ginger (*adrak*) paste	1 3/4 tsp	crushed	1/4 tsp	
Garlic (*lasan*) paste	1 3/4 tsp	Lemon juice	1 tsp	
Lemon (*nimbu*) juice	1 tsp	Green coriander (*hara dhaniya*),		
Turmeric (*haldi*) powder	1 tsp	finely chopped	1/4 cup	
Red chilli powder	1 tsp	**Step III:**		
Salt to taste		Yoghurt (*dahi*)	3/4 cup	
Cooking oil for frying	4 cups	Garlic paste	1 3/4 tsp	
Step II:		Coriander (*dhaniya*) powder	2 tsp	
Ghee	1 3/4 tbsp	Red chilli powder	1 tsp	
Cumin (*jeera*) seeds	1 tsp	Turmeric powder	1 tsp	
Green chillies, deseeded, finely chopped	2	Ghee	1/4 cup	
Ginger, 1" piece, finely chopped	1	Cashew nuts, roasted, blended with		
Carrots (*gajar*), peeled, finely chopped	1/4 cup	water to a fine paste	20	
French beans, stringed, finely chopped	1/4 cup	Salt to taste		
Potatoes, medium-sized, boiled,		White pepper (*safed mirch*) powder	1/2 tsp	
peeled, mashed	3	Clove powder	1/2 tsp	
Cashew nuts (*kaju*), roasted, crushed	12	Rose petal (*gulaab pankhri*) powder	1/2 tsp	
Raisins (*kishmish*), finely chopped	12	Vegetable stock (see p. 13)	1/2 cup	
Salt to taste		Green coriander, chopped	1 tbsp	

Preparation and Cooking time: 1 hr. 45 min. Serves: 4

Method

Peel the bottle gourd, cut off both ends and scoop the insides with a peeler.

Mix the step I ingredients (except oil) in a bowl. Rub the paste both inside and outside the bottle gourd and keep aside for 30 minutes.

Heat the oil in a wok on medium heat; fry the bottle gourd for 4-5 minutes or until it rises to the surface. Increase heat to high and continue to fry until the gourd is golden brown and fully cooked. Remove to a strainer to drain excess oil. Retain oil for future use.

Heat the ghee (step II) in a pan on medium heat; add cumin seeds. When the seeds begin to pop, add green chillies and ginger; stir well. Add carrots and beans; stir for 1 minute. Add mashed potatoes, stir, add cashew nuts and raisins; mix well. Add the remaining ingredients of step II and continue to stir and roast until the moisture dries up. Remove to a bowl and set aside to cool.

Once cool, stuff the bottle gourd with the filling.

Mix the yoghurt (step III) with garlic, coriander, red chilli, and turmeric powders.

Heat the ghee in a pan on medium heat; add the yoghurt mixture and stir and roast until fat appears on the sides. Add the cashew paste and salt and continue to stir and roast until fat appears on the sides.

Add the remaining ingredients (except green coriander) and stir and roast until the mixture is thick and homogenous.

Preheat oven to 180°C / 350°F. Arrange the stuffed gourd on an ovenproof serving platter. Pour the gravy over it and heat in the oven for 5-7 minutes. Remove, garnish with green coriander and serve.

Tempered Yoghurt

Dahi Chonkdaar

*Hung yoghurt (dahi)	900 gm / 2 lb		Green chillies, finely chopped	4
Olive oil	6 tbsp		Tomatoes, medium-sized, finely chopped	2
Cumin (jeera) seeds	1½ tsp		Turmeric (haldi) powder	2 tsp
Black mustard seeds (rai)	2 tsp		Salt to taste	
Garlic (lasan), finely chopped	3 tsp		Coriander (dhaniya) seeds, pounded	3 tsp
Onion, medium-sized, finely chopped	1		Black peppercorns (sabut kaali mirch),	
Curry leaves (kari patta)	24		freshly pounded	1½ tsp
Dry red chillies (sookhi lal mirch)	4		Salt to taste	
Ginger (adrak), finely chopped	1 tsp			

Method

Heat the olive oil in a pan on medium heat; add cumin and mustard seeds, sauté for 3-4 seconds or until the seeds begin to pop. Add garlic and sauté until light golden brown.

Add onion and sauté until light golden brown. Add curry leaves and dry red chillies, stir. Mix in ginger and green chillies. Add tomatoes and turmeric powder; roast for a minute. Add salt; stir. Add coriander seeds and black pepper; continue to stir and roast until fat appears on the sides.

Add yoghurt, stir until the masala and yoghurt have mixed completely. Check seasoning. Remove from heat.

Transfer to a bowl and serve at room temperature.

*Note: Tie yoghurt in a muslin cloth and hang overnight. The end product after the water has been reduced is hung yoghurt.

35

Stir-fried Vegetables with Coriander
Subzi Chonkdaar

Baby corn (*bhutta*), cut diagonally into 1½″ pieces	12	Coriander (*dhaniya*) seeds, crushed	3 tsp
		Red chilli powder	1 tsp
Champignon mushrooms (*khumb*), medium-sized, cut into halves	6	Tomato purée	6 tbsp
Red bell pepper, medium-sized, cut into thick strips	1	Black peppercorns (*sabut kaali mirch*), crushed	1 tsp
		Salt to taste	
Broccoli, medium-sized, florets removed, stalks discarded	1	Cumin (*jeera*) powder, roasted	1 tsp
		Dry fenugreek leaf (*kasoori methi*) powder	½ tsp
Asparagus, cut into 3″ pieces	6	Green coriander (*hara dhaniya*), finely chopped	1 tbsp
Cooking oil	4 tbsp		
Garlic (*lasan*) cloves, finely chopped	12	Lemon (*nimbu*) juice	1 tsp
Onion, medium-sized, finely chopped	1	Ginger (*adrak*), 1″ piece, cut into fine juliennes	1

Method

Heat the oil in a wok on medium heat; add garlic and sauté until golden brown.

Add onion and stir and roast until light golden brown.

Increase heat to high, add all the vegetables except broccoli and asparagus; stir-fry for 3-4 minutes.

Reduce heat to low, add coriander seeds and red chilli powder, stir. Add tomato purée, stir-fry for 1-2 minutes. Add broccoli and asparagus, stir for a minute.

Add black pepper, salt, cumin and dry fenugreek leaf powders; stir for a minute. Add green coriander and lemon juice; stir for a minute mixing the vegetables and the spices well. Adjust the seasoning and remove from heat.

Transfer to a bowl and serve garnished with ginger.

Cumin-flavoured Potatoes

Jeera Aloo

Preparation and Cooking time: 45 min. Serves: 4

Baby potatoes, washed well and shaken dry	350 gm / 12 oz	Turmeric (*haldi*) powder	1/2 tsp
Cooking oil	4 tbsp	Red chilli powder	1 tsp
Cumin (*jeera*) seeds	1 1/2 tsp	Tomato purée	2 tbsp
Asafoetida (*hing*), dissolved in 2 tbsp water	2 pinches	White pepper (*safed mirch*) powder	1/2 tsp
Ginger (*adrak*), finely chopped	1 tsp	Dry mango powder (*amchur*)	1 tsp
Green chillies, medium-sized, finely chopped	3	Dry fenugreek leaf (*kasoori methi*) powder	1/2 tsp
Salt to taste		Cumin powder, roasted	1 tsp
Coriander (*dhaniya*) powder	1 tsp	Lemon (*nimbu*) juice	1 tsp
		Ginger, 1" piece, cut into fine juliennes	1

Method

Boil the potatoes in 4 cups of water with 1 tbsp salt until fully cooked. Peel and keep aside. Discard the water.

Heat the oil in a wok on medium heat; add cumin seeds and asafoetida. When the seeds begin to pop, add ginger and green chillies; stir and add potatoes. Stir and roast for a minute.

Add salt, coriander, turmeric, and red chilli powders. Continue to stir and roast for 1-2 minutes. Add tomato purée and roast until specks of fat start appearing on the sides.

Add the white pepper, mango, fenugreek, and cumin powders; stir and add lemon juice, roast on high heat for 1-2 minutes and remove from heat.

Transfer to a bowl and serve garnished with ginger.

Lamb and Whole Spice Curry

Khadey Masaley ka Gosht

Preparation and Cooking time: 1 hr. 50 min. Serves: 4

Single lamb chops with bones, cut into 2″ length	225 gm / ½ lb	Black peppercorns (*sabut kaali mirch*)	12
Ghee	½ cup	Ginger (*adrak*) paste	3¼ tsp
Green cardamom (*choti elaichi*)	6	Garlic (*lasan*) paste	4 tsp
Black cardamom (*badi elaichi*)	2	Salt to taste	
Cinnamon (*dalchini*), 1″ sticks	4	Coriander powder	2 tsp
Cloves (*laung*)	4	Turmeric (*haldi*) powder	1¾ tsp
Bay leaves (*tej patta*), medium-sized	2	Red chilli powder	1 tsp
Onions, thinly sliced	1¼ cups	Yoghurt (*dahi*), whisked	½ cup
Cumin (*jeera*) seeds	1½ tsp	Dry fenugreek leaf (*kasoori methi*) powder	1 tsp
Coriander (*dhaniya*) seeds	5 tsp	Green coriander (*hara dhaniya*), finely chopped	4 tbsp
Dry red chillies (*sookhi lal mirch*)	4	Ginger, 1″ piece, cut into fine juliennes	1

Method

Heat the ghee in a pot on medium heat; add both cardamoms, cinnamon sticks, cloves, and bay leaves; stir for a minute. Add onions and stir and roast until onions turn golden brown. Add cumin and coriander seeds, dry red chillies, and black peppercorns; increase heat and stir for a minute.

Stir in the lamb and sear for a minute on high heat. Add ginger-garlic paste and salt; stir and roast for a minute. Add ½ cup of water (or lamb stock, see p. 13) and bring to the boil. Reduce heat to medium; add coriander, turmeric, and red chilli powders, stir. Reduce heat to low, cover and simmer for 3-4 minutes. Remove cover, increase heat to medium and stir and roast until fat appears on the sides.

Add yoghurt and continue to stir and roast until fat appears on the sides. Finally add 1½ cups of water (or lamb stock) and dried fenugreek powder, stir, cover and simmer on low heat for 12-15 minutes or until the lamb is tender and fully cooked.

Increase heat to high, add green coriander and stir and roast until fat just starts to appear on the sides. Remove from heat.

Transfer to a bowl and serve garnished with ginger.

Black Pepper Stewed Lamb Chops

Chaamp Kaali Mirch

Preparation and Cooking time: 1 hr. 40 min. Serves: 4

Lamb chops	12 pieces	Almonds (*badaam*), roasted, peeled,	
Step I:		blended with water to make	
Lemon (*nimbu*) juice	3 tbsp	a fine paste	2 tbsp
Garlic (*lasan*) paste	3¹/₄ tsp	Yoghurt (*dahi*)	¹/₂ cup
Ginger (*adrak*) paste	2¹/₂ tsp	Lamb stock (see p. 13)	1¹/₂ cups
Red chilli powder	2 tsp	Salt to taste	
Green cardamom (*choti elaichi*)		Black peppercorns (*sabut kaali mirch*),	
powder	¹/₂ tsp	freshly ground	1¹/₂ tsp
Nutmeg (*jaiphal*) powder	¹/₂ gm	Dry fenugreek leaf (*kasoori methi*)	
Salt to taste		powder	1¹/₂ tsp
Step II:		Rose petal (*gulaab pankhri*) powder	¹/₂ tsp
Ghee	6 tbsp	Clove (*laung*) powder	a pinch
Garlic, finely chopped	1¹/₂ tbsp	Mint (*pudina*) leaves, finely chopped	2 tsp
Black cumin (*shahi jeera*) seeds	¹/₂ tsp	Green coriander (*hara dhaniya*),	
Coriander (*dhaniya*) powder	1¹/₂ tsp	finely chopped	1¹/₂ tbsp
Red chilli powder	1 tsp	Cream	2 tbsp

Method

Mix the step 1 ingredients with the lamb. Rub the marinade well on each chop and keep aside for a minimum of 45 minutes. to a maximum of 4-6 hours.

Preheat the oven to 180°C / 350°F. Brush the chops with oil and bake on a roasting tray for 30-35 minutes or until succulent and fully cooked. Discard the residue and retain the lamb chops.

Heat the ghee (step II) in a pan on medium heat; add garlic and sauté till golden brown. Add black cumin seeds, coriander and red chilli powders; stir and add almond paste. Stir and roast until fat appears on the sides. Add yoghurt and continue to stir until fat appears again.

Add lamb stock (or water) and bring to the boil. Reduce heat to low and gently lower the chops in the pan. Add salt, black pepper, fenugreek, rose petal, and clove powders; stir gently.

Cover and simmer on low heat for 2-3 minutes. Remove cover, add mint and green coriander. Increase heat to medium and stir gently, taking care not to break the chops, until the consistency of the liquid becomes thick. Stir in the cream gently. Adjust the seasoning and remove and serve garnished with freshly ground black peppercorns.

Lamb Qorma with Cardamom

Rampuri Gosht Qorma

Preparation and Cooking time: 1hr. 45 min. Serves: 4

Lamb shoulder, boneless, cut into 2" cubes	450 gm / 1 lb	Yoghurt (*dahi*)	1/2 cup
Ghee	9 tbsp	Red chilli powder	1 1/2 tsp
Green cardamom (*choti elaichi*)	6	Cashew nuts (*kaju*), roasted, blended with water to make a fine paste	18
Cinnamon (*dalchini*), 1" sticks	2		
Cloves (*laung*)	4	Lamb stock (see p. 13)	2 cups
Onions, thinly sliced	1 1/4 cups	Green cardamom powder	1 tsp
Ginger (*adrak*) paste	1 tsp	Black pepper (*kaali mirch*) powder	1/2 tsp
Garlic (*lasan*) paste	2 tsp	Mace (*javitri*) powder	a pinch
Salt to taste		Rose water (*gulaab jal*)	5 drops
Coriander (*dhaniya*) powder	2 tsp	Saffron (*kesar*), soaked in 1 tbsp water	1/2 tsp

Method

Heat the ghee in a pot and set to medium heat; add green cardamom, cinnamon sticks, and cloves and sauté until cardamom changes colour. Add onions and stir and roast until they turn golden brown. Add the lamb, increase heat and stir and roast for a minute.

Reduce heat to medium, add ginger-garlic pastes and salt; stir well. Add coriander powder; stir and roast until fat appears on the sides. Add yoghurt and red chilli powder; continue to stir and roast until fat appears again. Add cashew nut paste and stir and roast until fat appears on the sides again.

Add lamb stock (or water) and bring to the boil. Reduce heat and cook covered, stirring occasionally until the lamb is fully cooked.

Remove from heat and pick out the lamb pieces from the pot into a new pan. Sprinkle green cardamom, black pepper and mace powders, rose water, and saffron. Strain the gravy through a fine mesh soup strainer into the pan. Bring to the boil, adjust the seasoning and remove from heat.

Transfer to a bowl and serve.

Leg of Lamb with Nutmeg
Raan Jaiphali

Leg of lamb	1 (1 1/2-2 kg / 3.3-4.4 lb)	Onion, medium-sized, roughly sliced	1
Step I:		Water	2 cups
Malt vinegar (*sirka*)	3 tbsp	**Step III:**	
Garlic (*lasan*) paste	1 1/2 tbsp	Mustard oil	2 tbsp
Ginger (*adrak*) paste	1 tbsp	Hung yoghurt (*dahi*)	1/2 cup
Kachri powder	2 tbsp	Nutmeg powder	1/4 tsp
Red chilli powder	1 tbsp	Red chilli powder	1 tsp
Nutmeg (*jaiphal*) powder	1/2 tsp	Black cardamom (*badi elaichi*) powder	1/4 tsp
Salt to taste		Black pepper (*kaali mirch*) powder	1/2 tsp
Mustard (*sarson*) oil	1 tbsp	Cumin (*jeera*) powder	1 tsp
Step II:		Salt to taste	
Butter	1/4 cup	**Step IV:**	
Bay leaves (*tej patta*)	2	Lemon (*nimbu*) juice	1 tbsp
Ginger, 1" piece, coarsely chopped	1	Onions, cut into rings	2
Garlic cloves, roughly chopped	10		

Preparation and Cooking time: 5 1/2 hrs. Serves: 4

Method

Wash the lamb thigh well, shake dry and keep in strainer to drain excess water. Take a thick fork and poke the leg in several places to make small holes.

Mix the step I ingredients in a bowl and rub this mixture over the lamb. Keep aside for a minimum of 4 hours.

Preheat the oven to 180°C / 350°F. Mix the step II ingredients on a roasting tray. Place the lamb thigh on the tray and cover with silver foil. Roast the lamb for 40-45 minutes, flipping it over once during this time. Add more water, if required. Check lamb by inserting a knife through it. If the lamb is cooked the knife will move easily and no raw residue will stick on it. Remove from the oven and set aside to cool.

Mix the step III ingredients on a flat tray. Rub this mixture over the lamb making sure it coats the entire thigh. Reserve for 30 minutes. Place the lamb thigh on a greased tray and roast again for 8-10 minutes. Alternatively, the lamb can also be grilled on a charcoal grill.

Transfer on to a platter and serve sprinkled with lemon juice and garnished with onion rings.

47

Lamb Cooked with Grams
Daal Gosht

Preparation and Cooking time: 1 hr. 50 min. Serves: 4

Lamb shanks, with bone, cut into 2" length	450 gm / 1 lb	Turmeric (*haldi*) powder	2 tsp
Bengal gram (*chana daal*), washed well, soaked overnight	3/4 cup	Red chilli powder	1 1/2 tsp
		Salt to taste	
Husked lentil (*masoor*), soaked for 30 minutes	75 gm / 2 1/2 oz	Water	1/2 cup
		Green chillies, deseeded, finely chopped	4
Ghee	8 tbsp	Ginger, finely chopped	1 1/2 tsp
Green cardamom (*choti elaichi*)	4	Green coriander (*hara dhaniya*)	2 1/2 tbsp
Black cardamom (*badi elaichi*)	2	Mint (*pudina*) leaves	1/4 cup
Cinnamon (*dalchini*), 1" sticks	2	Lemon (*nimbu*) juice	2 tbsp
Bay leaves (*tej patta*), medium-sized	2	Cream	4 tbsp
Cumin (*jeera*) seeds	1 1/2 tsp	Black cardamom powder	1/2 tsp
Onions, thinly sliced	1 1/2 cups	Cinnamon powder	a pinch
Ginger (*adrak*) paste	1 3/4 tsp	Cumin seeds, roasted, powdered	1 1/2 tsp
Garlic (*lasan*) paste	4 tsp	Clove (*laung*) powder	a pinch
Coriander (*dhaniya*) powder	2 tsp	Black pepper (*kaali mirch*) powder	1/2 tsp
		Rose petal (*gulaab pankhri*) powder	1/2 tsp

Method

Heat the ghee in a pot on medium heat; add both cardamoms, cinnamon sticks, bay leaves, and cumin seeds; stir till the seeds begin to pop. Add the onions and stir and roast until they turn golden brown. Remove 1/4 of the onions and keep aside.

Add lamb and sear on high heat for about a minute. Stir in the ginger and garlic pastes. Add coriander, turmeric, and red chilli powders, and salt; stir. Add water, stir, reduce heat and cover and simmer for 5 minutes, stirring occasionally. Increase heat and stir and roast until fat appears on the sides.

Add the daals; mix well. Add 6 cups of water, bring to the boil, reduce heat and cover and simmer for 20-25 minutes. Do not stir the mixture. Remove cover, and mix in green chillies, ginger, green coriander, and mint. Add lemon juice and stir well. Mix in the cream. Add the remaining ingredients and continue to stir on medium-low heat until the lamb is fully cooked and the daal and water form a homogenous mixture.

Transfer to a bowl and serve garnished with the reserved onions.

Lamb Brains with Black Pepper

Magaz Masala Kaali Mirch

Step I:

Lamb brains, medium sized	6 pieces
Water	3 cups
Turmeric (*haldi*) powder	1 tsp
Red chilli powder	1 tsp
Ginger (*adrak*) paste	1³/₄ tsp
Garlic (*lasan*) paste	2¹/₂ tsp
Salt to taste	
Lemon (*nimbu*) juice	1 tbsp

Step II:

Butter	4 tbsp
Garlic, finely chopped	5 tsp
Onions, finely chopped	¹/₂ cup
Black cumin (*shahi jeera*) seeds	¹/₂ tsp
Ginger, finely chopped	1 tsp
Green chillies, finely chopped	1 tsp
Tomato purée	¹/₂ cup
Turmeric powder	¹/₂ tsp
Salt to taste	
Black peppercorns (*sabut kaali mirch*), freshly ground	¹/₂ tbsp
Dry fenugreek leaf (*kasoori methi*) powder	1 tsp
Cream	2 tbsp
Green coriander (*hara dhaniya*), finely chopped	2 tbsp

Method

Heat the water (step I) in a pan; add turmeric and red chilli powders, ginger-garlic pastes, salt and lemon juice; bring to the boil. Add the brains gently into the water taking care not to break them. Boil for 20-25 minutes. Remove the brains gently and transfer to a bowl of iced water. Discard the water used for boiling.

Heat the butter (step II) in a pan on medium heat; sauté the garlic until golden brown. Add onions and continue to sauté until light golden brown.

Add black cumin seeds, ginger, and green chillies; stir and add tomato purée and turmeric powder. Continue to stir and roast on medium heat until fat appears on the sides.

Add the brain, salt, and ¹/₂ cup of water (or lamb stock, see p. 13); continue to stir and roast gently, taking care not to mash the brain too much (small chunks should remain). Cook until the moisture almost dries up.

Add the black pepper and fenugreek powder; mix well. Stir in the cream and green coriander. Remove from heat.

Transfer to a bowl and serve.

Chicken Breasts in Coconut Milk

Murgh Sunheri Nariyalwaala

Preparation and Cooking time: 1 hr. 15 min. Serves: 4

Chicken breasts	8	Cinnamon (*dalchini*), 1" sticks	2
Step I:		Garlic (*lasan*) cloves, chopped	20
Groundnuts (*moongphalli*), roasted,		Onions, finely chopped	1/2 cup
peeled	30 gm / 1 oz	Salt to taste	
Coriander (*dhaniya*) seeds	1 tbsp	Green cardamom powder	1 tsp
Dry red chillies (*sookhi lal mirch*)	2	Black pepper (*kaali mirch*) powder	1/2 tsp
Coconut (*nariyal*), desiccated	2 tbsp	Mace (*javitri*) powder	a pinch
Cumin (*jeera*) powder	1 1/2 tsp	Clove (*laung*) powder	a pinch
Turmeric (*haldi*) powder	1 tsp	Lemon (*nimbu*) juice	1 tbsp
Ginger (*adrak*), peeled	2 1/2 tbsp	Coconut milk powder, mixed with	
Step II:		1/3 cup hot water	1/4 cup
Ghee	6 tbsp	or Fresh coconut milk (see p. 13)	1/2 cup
Green cardamom (*choti elaichi*)	6	Green chillies, deseeded, cut into juliennes	2

Method

Mix the step I ingredients (except turmeric powder and ginger) in a pan and dry roast on medium heat for a few minutes or until the ingredients change colour to light brown. Cool, mix with a little water and blend with ginger and turmeric powder to a fine paste.

Heat the ghee (step II) in a pot; set to medium heat and add green cardamom and cinnamon sticks; stir until cardamom changes colour. Add garlic and stir until light golden brown. Add onions and stir and roast until light golden brown. Add 1/2 cup of water (or chicken stock, see p. 13) and continue to stir until all the moisture dries up and the fat appears on the sides.

Add the gravy paste from step I, stir and roast until the fat appears on the sides.

Add the chicken and salt; stir and roast until fat appears on the sides. Add 1 cup of water (or chicken stock), green cardamom, black pepper, mace and clove powders, cover, increase heat and bring to the boil. Reduce heat and simmer for 2-3 minutes or until the chicken is fully cooked. Remove the cover, add lemon juice, stir for a minute, add coconut milk and bring to the boil. Remove from heat.

Transfer to a bowl and serve garnished with green chillies.

Home-style Chicken Curry

Shorbeydaar Murgh

Preparation and Cooking time: 45 min. Serves: 4

Chicken thighs, with bone	8	Cumin (*jeera*) powder	1 tsp
Ghee	6 tbsp	Red chilli powder	1 tsp
Cinnamon (*dalchini*), 1" sticks	4	Black peppercorns (*sabut kaali mirch*),	
Garlic (*lasan*) cloves, finely chopped	24	freshly ground	1 tsp
Onion, large, finely chopped	1	Chicken stock (see p. 13)	5 cups
Ginger (*adrak*), finely chopped	1½ tbsp	Cinnamon powder	½ tsp
Green chillies, finely chopped	4	Lemon (*nimbu*) juice	1 tbsp
Salt to taste		Green coriander (*hara dhaniya*),	
Turmeric (*haldi*) powder	1 tsp	finely chopped	2 tbsp
Coriander (*dhaniya*) powder	1½ tsp		

Method

Wash the chicken, shake dry and reserve in a strainer to drain excess water.

Heat the ghee in a pot on medium heat; add cinnamon sticks, stir. Add garlic and stir and roast until light golden brown.

Add onion and stir and roast until light golden brown. Add ginger and green chillies, stir for 30 seconds. Add chicken and increase heat to high. Add salt, turmeric, coriander, cumin, and red chilli powders; stir and roast until fat starts to appear on the sides.

Add black pepper and chicken stock; stir. Increase heat and bring to the boil. Cover and simmer on low heat for 3-4 minutes, stirring occasionally.

Remove cover, add cinnamon powder, lemon juice, and green coriander. Continue to stir and cook for 1-2 minutes, adjust the seasoning and remove.

Chicken & Fennel Pilaf

Murgh Pulao Saunfia

Basmati rice, washed		Yoghurt (*dahi*), whisked well	1/2 cup
soaked for 45 minutes	340 gm / 12 oz	Onion, medium-sized, thinly sliced	1
Step 1:		**Step II:**	
Chicken breasts, boneless,		Ghee	1/2 cup
cut into 2" cubes	450 gm / 1 lb	Chicken stock (see p. 13)	3 cups
Salt to taste		Salt to taste	
Garlic (*lasan*) paste	1 1/2 tbsp	Green chillies, slit lengthwise	
Ginger (*adrak*) paste	1 tbsp	into two, deseeded	4
Fennel (*moti saunf*) powder	2 tbsp	Ginger, 1" piece, cut into juliennes	1
White pepper (*safed mirch*) powder	1 tsp	Lemon (*nimbu*) juice	1 tsp
Green cardamom (*choti elaichi*) powder	1 tsp	Cream, single	1/2 cup

Method

Mix the step 1 ingredients together. Keep aside for 30 minutes.

Heat the ghee (step II) in a pot on medium heat; add the above mixture and stir and roast until fat appears on the sides.

Add chicken stock (or water) and bring the mixture to the boil. Check if chicken is cooked. Strain the rice, discard the soaking water and slowly transfer the rice into the pot, stirring gently.

Add salt, green chillies, ginger, and lemon juice, stir gently. Simmer gently for 10-12 minutes, stirring occasionally. Check the seasoning and add more salt if required.

Press a grain of rice between the fingers to see if fully cooked. Add more stock or water, if necessary.

When the water is on the verge of drying up, reduce heat to very low, add the cream, stirring very gently taking care not to mash the rice. Cover and simmer on very low heat for 3-4 minutes. If it is difficult to achieve very low heat, a griddle can be used as a medium between the pot and the burner.

Transfer on to a rice platter and serve.

Preparation and Cooking time: 1 hr. 45 min. Serves: 4

55

Lamb Rice with Biryani

Gosht Dum Biryani

Lamb shoulder, boneless, cut into 2″ cubes	225 gm / ¹/₂ lb
Lamb chops	8
Step I:	
Garlic (*lasan*) paste	1¹/₂ tbsp
Ginger (*adrak*) paste	1 tbsp
Salt to taste	
Red chilli powder	1 tsp
Yoghurt (*dahi*), whisked	¹/₂ cup
Ghee	¹/₂ cup
Green cardamom (*choti elaichi*)	6
Black cardamom (*badi elaichi*)	2
Cloves (*laung*)	4
Cinnamon (*dalchini*), 1″ sticks	2
Bay leaves (*tej patta*)	2
Onions, medium-sized, thinly sliced	2
Water	3 cups
Lemon (*nimbu*) juice	1 tbsp
Green cardamom powder	1 tsp

Mace (*javitri*) powder	¹/₂ tsp
Cream	3 tbsp
Step II:	
Basmati rice, washed few times, soaked for 25 minutes	225 gm / ¹/₂ lb
Water	6 cups
Salt to taste	
Green cardamom	4
Cinnamon, 1″ stick	1
Cloves	2
Rose water (*gulaab jal*)	1 tsp
Lemon juice	1 tsp
Step III:	
Ginger, 1″ piece, cut into juliennes	1
Green chillies, medium-sized, deseeded, cut into juliennes	3
Mint (*pudina*) leaves	18
Saffron (*kesar*), soaked in 1 tbsp water	¹/₂ tsp
Ghee	2 tbsp

Method

Mix the garlic-ginger pastes, salt, red chilli powder, and yoghurt in a bowl using a whisk.

Heat the ghee in a pan on medium heat; add both cardamoms, cloves, cinnamon sticks, and bay leaves; sauté for a minute. Add onions and stir and roast until golden brown. Remove one third of the browned onions and keep aside in a strainer or absorbent paper to remove excess oil.

Add the lamb, increase heat to high, sear for 1-2 minutes, reduce heat to medium and continue to stir and roast until fat appears on the sides.

Add the yoghurt mixture and stir and roast until fat starts to appear on the sides.

Add water, increase heat to high and bring to the boil. Reduce heat to low, cover and simmer, stirring occasionally for 30-35 minutes or until the lamb is tender. Add more water if required (two third amount of water must be left).

Remove from heat and keep aside to cool. Once cool, pick out the lamb pieces from the gravy using a spoon or tongs. Strain the gravy through a soup strainer. Retain the gravy and discard the pulp. Add the lamb pieces back to the gravy with the lemon juice. Mix well, add green cardamom and mace powders and cream; mix again. Keep aside.

Add the water (step II) for the rice in a new pot. Add salt. The water should taste extra salty. Add green cardamom, cinnamon stick, cloves, rose water, and lemon juice; bring to the boil on high heat. Now add the rice, reduce heat to medium and continue to cook, stirring very gently until rice is almost but not fully cooked. Strain the rice and drain the water.

Heat the strained gravy in a pot on high heat and bring to the boil. Reduce heat to very low, transfer half the rice in the gravy. Sprinkle half the ginger, green chillies, and mint leaves over the rice. Repeat the process again. Finally spread the ghee and the saffron over the top of the rice. Cover and cook for 4-5 minutes. If it is difficult to achieve very low heat, a griddle can be used as a medium between the pot and the burner.

Remove from heat, transfer to a rice platter and garnish with the reserved fried onions. Serve immediately.

Roasted Vermicelli Cooked in Milk

Meethi Sevain

Semolina vermicelli	225 gm / $^1/_2$ lb	Coconut (*nariyal*), desiccated	3 tbsp
Milk	4 cups	Water	$^1/_2$ cup
Cinnamon (*dalchini*), 1″ sticks	2	Cinnamon powder	$^1/_2$ tsp
Sugar	8 tbsp	Almond (*badaam*) flakes	3 tbsp
Ghee	$^1/_4$ cup	Dried dates (*khajoor*), cut into juliennes	12

Method

Heat the milk in a pot on medium heat. Add cinnamon sticks and bring to the boil. Add sugar and stir until it dissolves completely. Strain to a new bowl.

Heat the ghee in a pan on medium heat. Add vermicelli and coconut and stir and roast until vermicelli is golden brown. Mix in the water; add cinnamon powder, stir and reduce heat to low. Add the milk mixture, increase heat to medium and continue to simmer for 3-4 minutes, stirring occasionally.

Transfer to a bowl and serve garnished with almond flakes and dried dates. Serve at room temperature.

Preparation and Cooking time: 45 min. Serves: 4

Green Coriander: Hara Dhaniya

Very strong and pleasantly aromatic

Mint: Pudina

Pure and refreshing odour,
pungent and burning taste

Dill: Sooya

Sweet fragrance, especially
when fresh

Curry Leaves: Kari Patta

Fresh and pleasant and remotely
reminiscent of oranges

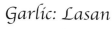

Coconut: Nariyal

Pleasant, mild and nutty fragrance,
with a hint of sweetness

Garlic: Lasan

Strong and characteristic odour,
which is markedly different
in fresh and fried state

fresh herbs and vegetables

Tomato & Fresh Coriander Soup
Tamater ka Shorba Dhaniyawaala

Preparation and Cooking time: 1 hr. 10 min. Serves: 4

Tomatoes, cut into quarters	900 gm / 2 lb	Garlic (*lasan*) cloves	12
Butter	5 tsp	Green coriander (*hara dhaniya*), leaves	
Cumin (*jeera*) seeds	3 tsp	& stems separated & chopped	5 tbsp
Green cardamom (*choti elaichi*)	4	Black peppercorns (*sabut kaali mirch*)	12
Black cardamom (*badi elaichi*)	2	Kashmiri red chilli powder	1 tsp
Cinnamon (*dalchini*), 1″ sticks	2	Water	4 cups
Bay leaves (*tej patta*)	2	White pepper (*safed mirch*)	
Salt to taste		powder	1/2 tsp
Ginger (*adrak*), coarsely chopped	1 1/2 tsp	Cumin seeds, roasted, powdered	1 1/2 tsp

Method

Heat the butter in a pan on medium heat; add cumin seeds, both cardamoms, cinnamon sticks, and bay leaves; stir. Add tomatoes and salt; stir.

Add ginger, garlic, green coriander stems, black peppercorns, and red chilli powder; stir. Add water, increase heat and bring the mixture to the boil. Reduce heat, cover and simmer for 30 minutes.

Remove from heat and strain into a separate pot using a soup strainer.

Bring the strained mixture to the boil. Boil for 2-3 minutes. Add white pepper and cumin powders; stir and reduce heat to low. Add green coriander leaves, stir and simmer for 2-3 minutes.

Transfer to individual soup bowls and serve hot garnished with croutons (optional).

Coconut & Drumstick Soup
Nariyal aur Saijan ki Phalli ka Shorba

Drumsticks (*saijan ki phalli*), stringed, cut into 1" pieces	2	Ginger (*adrak*), finely chopped	1 tsp
Coconut (*nariyal*) oil	4 tbsp	Onions, medium-sized, thinly sliced	2
Garlic (*lasan*) cloves, finely chopped	10	Turmeric (*haldi*) powder	1 tsp
Dry red chillies (*sookhi lal mirch*)	2	Tomatoes, thinly sliced	2
Black mustard seeds (*rai*)	1 tsp	Salt to taste	
Curry leaves (*kari patta*)	24	Coconut milk powder, mixed with 2 cups of hot water	2 cups
Green chillies, finely chopped	2	Lemon (*nimbu*) juice	1 tbsp

Method

Boil the drumsticks in salted water, drain and reserve drumsticks.

Heat the coconut oil in a pan on medium heat; add garlic and sauté until it just starts to change colour. Add dry red chillies, mustard seeds, and curry leaves; stir.

Add green chillies and ginger; stir. Add onions and sauté for a minute until they turn glossy. Add turmeric powder and 1-2 tbsp water; sauté for a minute.

Add drumsticks, tomatoes, and salt. Gently simmer for a minute.

Add coconut milk, increase heat and bring to the boil. Reduce heat and simmer stirring gently for 2-3 minutes. Add lemon juice.

Transfer to individual soup bowls and serve garnished with fried curry leaves.

Preparation and Cooking time: **50 min.** *Serves:* **4**

Corn Kebabs

Makkai kebab

American corn kernels (canned)	1 can / 200 gm / 7 oz	Green chillies, medium-sized, deseeded, finely chopped	2
Processed cheese / Cheddar cheese, grated	1/2 cup	Dry mango powder (*amchur*)	1 tsp
Mint (*pudina*) leaves, fresh, finely chopped	1 tbsp	Black pepper (*kaali mirch*), freshly ground	1 tsp
Green coriander (*hara dhaniya*), finely chopped	2 tsp	Red chilli powder	1 tsp
Ginger (*adrak*), 1" piece, finely chopped	1	Cornflour	1 tbsp
Onion, medium-sized, finely chopped	1	Breadcrumbs	3 tbsp
		Salt to taste	
		Cooking oil	1/2 cup

Method

Mix all the ingredients together (except oil) until a dough-like mixture is formed. Add more cornflour or breadcrumbs to ensure the above consistency, if necessary.

Divide the mixture equally into 8 portions and shape each portion into 1"-thick, flat roundel. Place these roundels on a flat tray and keep aside.

Heat the oil to medium in a pan; shallow fry the roundels until light golden brown on both sides.

Transfer on to a platter and serve hot with mint chutney (see p. 13).

Jalapenos with Jaggery & Coconut
Hyderabadi Mirchi Saalan

Jalapeno chillies, poked with a sharp fork all over	16
Cooking oil	2 tbsp
Salt to taste	
White pepper (*safed mirch*) powder	1/2 tsp

Step I:

Groundnuts (*moongphalli*), roasted, peeled	1/2 cup
Desiccated coconut powder (*nariyal burada*)	4 tbsp
Sesame (*til*) seeds	1 1/2 tbsp
Coriander (*dhaniya*) seeds	1 tbsp
Cumin (*jeera*) seeds	2 tsp
Turmeric (*haldi*) powder	1 tsp
Black peppercorns (*sabut kaali mirch*), crushed	1/2 tsp

Dry red chillies (*sookhi lal mirch*)	4
Salt to taste	

Step II:

Ginger (*adrak*), 1" piece, roughly chopped	1
Garlic (*lasan*) cloves, finely chopped	8
Jaggery (*gur*), crushed	1 tbsp

Step III:

Water	1 1/2 cups
Tamarind (*imli*), soaked in 1/2 cup water for 1 hour	5 tbsp
Mustard (*sarson*) oil	2 tbsp
Mustard seeds (*rai*)	1 tsp
Cumin seeds	1/2 tsp
Black onion seeds (*kalonji*)	1/2 tsp
Curry leaves (*kari patta*)	12

Preparation and Cooking time: 1 hr. 35 min. Serves: 4

Method

Spread the chillies on a baking tray, drizzle with oil, salt, and white pepper powder. Roast in an oven at 120-150°C / 250-300°F for 10-12 minutes. Remove and cool.

Mix the step I ingredients in a pan, and dry roast the mixture on medium heat for a few minutes or until the ingredients change colour to light brown. Cool and grind to a fine powder in a dry grinder, then add a little water and blend with step II ingredients and make a smooth paste.

Mix the paste with 1 1/2 cups of water in a pot and cook on medium heat for 20-25 minutes or until the frothing stops and the mixture becomes homogenous. Add more water, if necessary.

Add the tamarind, stir and continue to cook for 5-6 minutes, stirring gently. Add the baked green chillies and stir. Remove from heat and transfer to a serving bowl.

Heat the mustard oil in a pan on medium heat; add mustard seeds, stir, add cumin and black onion seeds, stir for a minute. Add curry leaves. Remove and pour over the dish spreading evenly. Serve hot.

Cottage Cheese & Tomato
Tamater Paneer Hyderabadi

Cottage cheese (*paneer*)	225 gm / ½ lb
Tomatoes, cut into quarters	900 gm / 2 lb
Tamarind (*imli*), seedless, soaked in water for 1 hour	30 gm / 1 oz
Step I:	
Cooking oil	5 tsp
Cumin (*jeera*) seeds	1½ tsp
Green cardamom (*choti elaichi*)	4
Black cardamom (*badi elaichi*)	2
Cinnamon (*dalchini*), 1″ sticks	2
Salt to taste	
Onion, medium-sized, coarsely chopped	1
Ginger (*adrak*), coarsely chopped	6½ tsp
Curry leaves (*kari patta*)	18
Black peppercorns (*sabut kaali mirch*)	12

Kashmiri red chilli powder	2 tsp
Water	4 cups
Gram flour (*besan*), roasted	1½ tbsp
Step II:	
Coconut (*nariyal*) oil	2 tbsp
Garlic (*lasan*) cloves, finely chopped	12
Cumin seeds	1½ tsp
Black mustard seeds (*rai*)	1 tsp
Dry red chillies (*sookhi lal mirch*)	4
Curry leaves	12
Cherry tomatoes	12
Coconut milk powder, mixed well with ½ cup of hot water	½ cup
or Fresh coconut milk (see p. 13)	1 cup

Method

Boil the tamarind with water in a pan for 2-3 minutes. Remove from heat, cool and strain using a soup strainer. Keep the extract and discard the pulp.

Heat the oil (step 1) in a pot on medium heat; add cumin seeds, both cardamoms, and cinnamon sticks; stir. Add tomatoes and salt; stir. Add onion, ginger, curry leaves, black peppercorns, and red chilli powder; stir.

Add water and bring the mixture to the boil. Reduce heat to low, stir in the roasted gram flour, cover and simmer for 20-25 minutes. Remove from heat, strain using a soup strainer; keep aside.

Heat the coconut oil (step II) in a pan on medium heat; add garlic and sauté until golden brown. Add cumin, black mustard seeds, and dry red chillies; stir for 30 seconds. Add curry leaves, stir, add cherry tomatoes and stir for a minute.

Add the strained tomato gravy, increase heat to high and bring to the boil. Reduce heat to medium and mix in the tamarind water. Add cottage cheese and simmer for a minute. Add coconut milk and remove from heat as soon as the mixture comes to the boil.

Transfer to a bowl and serve.

Potatoes Roasted with Curry Leaves

Aloo Kari Patta

Baby potatoes, with skin, washed, peeled	32	Curry leaves (*kari patta*)		18
Step I:		Garlic (*lasan*) paste		2$^1/_2$ tsp
Coriander (*dhaniya*) seeds, crushed	I tbsp	Ginger (*adrak*) paste		2$^1/_2$ tsp
Cumin (*jeera*) seeds	2$^1/_2$ tsp	Turmeric (*haldi*) powder		$^1/_2$ tsp
Black peppercorns (*sabut kaali mirch*)	I2	Green chillies, medium-sized,		
Green cardamom (*choti elaichi*)	4	deseeded, finely chopped		4
Cloves (*laung*)	2	Lemon (*nimbu*) juice		I tsp
Cinnamon (*dalchini*), I" stick	I	Salt to taste		
Step II:		Green chillies, cut into juliennes		4
Cooking oil	3 tbsp	Tomatoes, medium-sized,		
Onions, medium-sized, finely chopped	3	cut into juliennes		I

Preparation and Cooking Time: 1 hr. 10 min. Serves: 4

Method

Dry roast the step I ingredients in a pan for approximately 2-3 minutes. Cool, blend to a fine powder and keep aside.

Heat the oil (step II) in a wok; add onions and sauté on medium heat until golden. Add curry leaves and sauté until they stop spluttering.

Add garlic and ginger pastes, stir; add turmeric powder and stir. Add potatoes and stir. Add green chillies and stir for a minute. Add the spice mix, stir and add $^1/_2$ cup of water; bring to the boil.

Reduce heat to medium and stir and roast until the water has almost dried up and the sauce covers the potatoes (approximately 2-3 minutes). Sprinkle lemon juice and stir. Remove and adjust the salt.

Transfer to a serving dish, garnish with green chillies, tomatoes, and onions.

Potato & Cauliflower with Fenugreek

Aloo Gobhi Methiwaali

Preparation and Cooking time: 50 min. Serves: 4

Cauliflower (*phool gobhi*), washed, cut into small florets	700 gm / 1½ lb	Cumin (*jeera*) seeds	1 tsp
Potatoes, large, washed, dried, chopped into 8 pieces with skin	2	Curry leaves (*kari patta*), washed, shaken dry	12
Fenugreek (*methi*) leaves, fresh, chopped	200 gm / 7 oz	Ginger (*adrak*), finely chopped	1 tsp
Cooking oil for frying		Salt to taste	
Mustard (*sarson*) oil	4 tbsp	Green chillies, medium-sized, finely chopped	2
Black mustard seeds (*rai*)	1 tsp	Dry mango powder (*amchur*)	1 tsp
		Lemon (*nimbu*) juice	1 tsp
		Pomegranate (*anaar*), fresh, peeled	30 gm / 1 oz

Method

Soak the florets in salt water for 5 minutes. Remove and wash again. (Alternatively, one can use a sterilizing solution). Keep aside in a strainer to drain the excess water.

Sprinkle and rub salt on the fenugreek leaves. Keep aside for 5 minutes and then wash in running water until all traces of salt have been removed. (This is done to reduce the bitterness of the fenugreek). Shake dry and keep aside.

Heat the oil in a wok; fry the potatoes on medium heat and then on high heat until fully cooked and with a crunchy and golden outer crust. Sprinkle with salt and keep aside.

Heat the mustard oil in a wok on high heat till it starts smoking. Reduce heat until smoking stops and oil reaches medium temperature. Add mustard seeds; after 2-3 seconds add cumin seeds and curry leaves. Mix in the ginger and fenugreek leaves; stir and roast on marginally increased heat for approximately 4-5 minutes or until the oil is visible on the sides.

Add cauliflower and salt; stir. Cook covered on low heat, stirring occasionally, for 3-4 minutes. Remove the cover, add green chillies and continue to stir and roast until the cauliflower is soft and the moisture has dried.

Increase heat, add potatoes and stir well. Add mango powder and lemon juice; cook for a minute. Remove from heat and serve hot garnished with fresh pomegranate.

Stuffed Potato Barrels

Bharwaan Aloo Khulley

Potatoes, large, washed, peeled	12	Cottage cheese (*paneer*), grated	1/2 cup
Cooking oil for deep-frying		Salt to taste	
Step I:		Cheddar cheese, grated	1 cup
Cooking oil	2 tbsp	Pomegranate (*anaar*), medium-sized, shelled	1
Cumin (*jeera*) seeds	1 tsp	Raisins (*kishmish*), roasted, chopped	6
Ginger (*adrak*), 1" piece, finely chopped	1	Green coriander (*hara dhaniya*), chopped	1 tsp
Green chillies, medium-sized,		Mint (*pudina*), fresh	1 tsp
deseeded, finely chopped	4	Wholemilk fudge (*khoya*)	1/4 cup
Dry mango powder (*amchur*)	2 tsp	**Step II:**	
Black pepper (*kaali mirch*), freshly ground	1 tsp	Refined flour (*maida*)	2 tbsp
Cumin powder	1/2 tsp	Cornflour	1 tbsp
Green cardamom (*choti elaichi*) powder	1/2 tsp	Cold water	1/2 cup
Nutmeg (*jaiphal*) powder	a pinch	Breadcrumbs	1 cup
Black rock salt (*kaala namak*)	a pinch	Cooking oil for deep-frying	

Preparation and Cooking time: 1 hr. 50 min. Serves: 4

Method

Scoop out the centre of the potatoes, leaving walls on the sides (should look like empty barrels). Heat the oil in a wok; deep-fry the potato barrels on medium heat until light golden brown. Remove and cool. Fry the scooped part until golden brown.

Heat the oil (step 1) to medium hot in a wok; add cumin seeds and sauté on medium heat until it begins to pop. Add ginger and green chillies; stir until lightly coloured.

Add mango, black pepper, cumin, green cardamom, and nutmeg powders; stir. Add rock salt and stir. Add cottage cheese and salt, stir and roast for 3-4 minutes. Remove and cool.

When cool, add cheese, pomegranate, raisins, green coriander, mint, and fried potato; mix well. Divide the mixture into 12 equal portions. Fill a portion of the filling in each potato barrel.

Mix the step II ingredients (except breadcrumbs and oil) to make a batter.

Dip the stuffed potato barrels into the batter, coat with breadcrumbs and fry on medium heat, turning at regular intervals, until golden. Remove to a strainer to drain excess oil. Cut each piece into half and serve hot.

Prawns with Curry Leaves

Jhinga Kari Patta

Step I:

Prawns, headless B grade, cleaned, washed, shelled	450 gm / 1 lb
Salt to taste	
Red chilli powder	1 tsp
Ginger (*adrak*) paste	½ tsp
Garlic (*lasan*) paste	1 tsp
Lemon (*nimbu*) juice	1 tbsp

Step II:

Mustard (*sarson*) oil	5 tbsp
Mustard seeds (*rai*)	2 tbsp
Garlic cloves, finely chopped	6

Curry leaves (*kari patta*)	18
Onion, medium-sized, finely chopped	1
Ginger, 1" piece, finely chopped	1
Green chillies, finely chopped	2
Tomato, medium-sized, finely chopped	1
Coconut milk powder, dissolved in ½ cup water	4 tbsp
or Fresh coconut milk (see p. 13)	½ cup
Black peppercorns (*sabut kaali mirch*), crushed	1 tsp
Salt to taste	

Method

Mix the step I ingredients in a bowl. Keep aside for minimum of 15 minutes to a maximum of 1 hour.

Heat the mustard oil (step II) in a pan on high heat till it starts smoking. Reduce heat until smoking stops and oil reaches medium temperature. Add mustard seeds; stir. Add garlic and continue to stir until light golden brown.

Add curry leaves and stir until the leaves become crisp.

Add onion and stir and roast until light golden brown. Add ginger, green chillies, and tomato. Stir and roast until fat starts to appear on the sides of the pan.

Add the marinated prawns, stir and roast for 2-3 minutes or until the prawns are fully cooked.

Add coconut milk, crushed black pepper, and salt; mix well. Cook for a minute. Check the seasoning and remove from heat.

Transfer to a serving bowl and serve hot.

Dill Infused Grilled Fish

Mahi Dill Se

Pink salmon fillet with skin, boneless, cut into 2" cubes	450 gm / 1 lb

Step 1:

Ginger (adrak) paste	1 tsp
Garlic (lasan) paste	2 tsp
Red chilli powder	1 tsp
Balsamic vinegar (sirka)	2 tbsp
Salt to taste	

Step II:

Mustard (sarson) oil	2 tbsp
Gram (besan) flour	1 tbsp
Fennel (moti saunf) powder	1/2 tsp
Dill (sooya) leaves, finely chopped	2 tbsp
Honey	2 tsp
*Hung yoghurt (dahi)	1/4 cup
Red chilli powder	1 tsp
Cream	2 tbsp
Lemon (nimbu) juice	1 tsp

Method

Wash the salmon, shake dry and keep in a strainer to drain excess water.

Mix the step 1 ingredients in a bowl. Add the salmon, mix well and keep aside for 1 hour.

In a flat mixing tray, mix mustard oil (step II) and gram flour together with the palm of your hand. Add fennel powder, dill leaves, honey, and yoghurt; mix well. Stir in red chilli powder and cream.

Transfer the fish to the tray and mix the marinade with the fish, ensuring that each cube gets well coated. Keep aside for 30 minutes.

Preheat oven to 180°C / 350°F. Bake on a roasting tray for 8-10 minutes or until the colour of the cubes changes to golden brown. Alternatively, the fish cubes can also be grilled on a charcoal grill.

Transfer the fish on to a serving platter and serve sprinkled with lemon juice.

*Note: Tie yoghurt in a muslin cloth and hang overnight. The end product after the water has been reduced is called hung yoghurt.

Chicken in Coriander Sauce

Murgh Qorma Dhaniyawaala

Preparation and Cooking time: 45 min. Serves: 4

Chicken thigh, boneless, cut into 2″ cubes	450 gm / 1 lb

Step I:

Yoghurt (*dahi*)	$^3/_4$ cup
Garlic (*lasan*) paste	$3^1/_4$ tsp
Ginger (*adrak*) paste	$1^3/_4$ tsp
Coriander (*dhaniya*) powder	1 tbsp
Turmeric (*haldi*) powder	$1^1/_2$ tsp
Red chilli powder	1 tsp
White pepper (*safed mirch*) powder	$^1/_2$ tsp

Step II:

Onions, medium-sized, peeled	3
Ghee	6 tbsp
Salt to taste	
Chicken stock (see p. 13)	2 cups
Green cardamom (*choti elaichi*) powder	1 tsp
Cinnamon (*dalchini*) powder	a pinch
Lemon (*nimbu*) juice	1 tsp
Cream, fresh	2 tbsp
Green coriander (*hara dhaniya*), finely chopped	1 cup

Method

Wash the chicken well, shake dry and keep in a strainer to drain excess water.

Mix the step I ingredients in a bowl with a whisk. Keep aside.

Boil the onions (step II) until cooked. Blend to a fine paste with 1 tbsp oil and some water.

Heat the ghee in a pot on medium heat; add the boiled onion paste and stir and roast until the moisture dries up and fat appears on the sides.

Add the step I mixture and stir and roast until fat appears on the sides.

Add chicken, increase heat to high, add salt and stir and roast till fat appears on the sides.

Add chicken stock and bring to the boil. Reduce heat, add green cardamom and cinnamon powders, lemon juice, and cream; stir. Add green coriander and cover and simmer for 2-3 minutes, stirring occasionally.

Remove from heat, transfer to a bowl and serve.

Chicken with Fresh Fenugreek
Methi Murgh

Chicken drumsticks, washed, shaken dry	8	Garlic, finely chopped	1 3/4 tbsp
Fenugreek (*methi*), fresh, chopped	225 gm / 1/2 oz	Onions, finely chopped	1/2 cup
Step I:		Salt to taste	
Salt to taste		Ginger, finely chopped	1 tsp
Lemon (*nimbu*) juice	2 tsp	Green chillies, medium-sized,	
White pepper (*safed mirch*) powder	1 tsp	finely chopped	2
Ginger (*adrak*) paste	1 3/4 tsp	Yoghurt (*dahi*)	1/2 cup
Black peppercorns (*sabut kaali mirch*),		Black cardamom (*badi elaichi*) powder	a pinch
freshly ground	1 1/4 tsp	Cinnamon (*dalchini*) powder	a pinch
Garlic (*lasan*) paste	1/2 tsp	Green coriander (*hara dhaniya*),	
Step II:		finely chopped	5 tbsp
Mustard (*sarson*) oil	5 tbsp	Lemon juice	1 tsp
Cumin (*jeera*) seeds	1 tsp	Ginger, 1" piece, cut into fine juliennes	1

Preparation and Cooking time: 1 hr. 25 min. Serves: 4

Method

Sprinkle and rub salt on the fenugreek leaves. Keep aside for 5 minutes and wash in running water until all traces of salt have been removed. (This is done to reduce the bitterness of the fenugreek). Shake dry and keep aside.

Mix the step I ingredients in a bowl and rub into the chicken. Keep aside.

Heat the mustard oil (step II) in a pan on high heat till it starts smoking. Reduce heat until smoking stops and oil reaches medium temperature. Add cumin seeds; when it splutters add garlic and sauté until golden brown. Add onions and sauté on medium heat until golden brown.

Add fenugreek leaves, and continue to stir and roast for approximately 4-5 minutes or until the oil appears on the sides. Add ginger and green chillies, stir. Stir in yoghurt and cook until the moisture is reduced and oil appears on the sides.

Add chicken, increase to high heat and sear for 2-3 minutes, reduce heat to medium and continue to cook until the chicken is fully cooked and oil appears on the sides. Add black cardamom and cinnamon powders, green coriander, and lemon juice; mix well. Remove from heat. Transfer to a bowl and serve garnished with ginger and fresh cream (optional).

Garlic-flavoured Yoghurt

Burrhani Raita

Preparation and Cooking time: 15-25 min. Serves: 4

Yoghurt (*dahi*)	500 gm / 1.1 lb	Black pepper (*kaali mirch*) powder	$1/2$ tsp
Garlic (*lasan*) paste	1 tbsp	Salt to taste	
Cumin (*jeera*) powder, roasted	$1 1/2$ tsp	Black rock salt (*kaala namak*)	$1/2$ tsp
Red chilli powder	$1/2$ tsp		

Method

Mix all the ingredients together in a bowl using a whisk or an egg beater.

Serve as an accompaniment to any Indian meal, particularly biryani and pulao.

Tender Coconut Pudding

Daab ka Meetha

Dried China grass (*agar agar*), 4" each	15	Lemon (*nimbu*) juice	1/2 tsp
Water	1/2 cup	Coconut milk powder, dissolved	
Condensed milk	1/2 cup	in 1/3 cup hot water	1/4 cup
Milk	1 cup	or Fresh coconut milk (see p. 13)	1/2 cup
Sugar	1/2 cup	Vanilla essence	1/2 tsp
Green coconut (*nariyal*), tender coconut		*Caramelized nuts, roughly chopped	1 tbsp
scooped out and roughly chopped	1		

Method

Soak the China grass in 1/2 cup of water for 15 minutes. Boil and stir until China grass dissolves fully in the water.

Mix condensed milk, milk, and sugar in a bowl and cook in a double boiler. Add tender coconut, lemon juice, and China grass liquid. Stir for a minute, add coconut milk and vanilla essence. Continue to stir until the mixture becomes thick.

Spread caramelized nuts in small pudding moulds and pour the mixture. Wait for the mixture to cool and refrigerate for a minimum of one hour.

Transfer the pudding from the moulds by gently turning them over serving dishes and serve.

Note: To make caramalized nuts—dry roast 1 tbsp cashew nuts (kaju) and 1 tbsp almonds (badaam) for 2-3 minutes in a pan. Remove and cool. In the same pan, add 2 tbsp sugar and cook on medium heat until it melts and starts turning brown. Add nuts, stir and remove to a lightly oiled tray to cool. Use as required.

Preparation and Cooking time: 30 min. Serves: 4

Dry Fenugreek Leaves: Kasoori Methi

Bitter and aromatic;
adds zest to many dishes

Onion Seeds: Kalonji

Aromatic and slightly bitter,
with little odour

Saffron: Kesar

Intensively fragrant and
slightly bitter in taste

Poppy Seeds: Khus Khus

Nutty and pleasant

Dry Pomegranate Seeds: Anaar dana

Fresh, sweet-sour with
pleasant taste

Sesame Seeds: *Til*

Tastes nutty, its flavour is
dramatically increased
by roasting

Mustard Seeds: *Rai*

Pungent and bitter taste with no
fragrance but when roasted the
seeds have a rich, nutty odour

Dry Rose Petals: *Gulaab Pankhri*

Flowery, perfume-like,
sweet and very pleasant

Fenugreek Seeds: *Methi Dana*

Bitter and aromatic

dried herbs, seeds and leaves

Fenugreek-flavoured Chargrilled Fish
Macchi Tikka Methiwaala

Preparation and Cooking time: 1 hr. 25 min. Serves: 4

Sole, fillets	450 gm / 1 lb	Dry fenugreek leaf (*kasoori methi*)	
Step I:		powder	1 tbsp
Malt vinegar (*sirka*)	3 tsp	Processed cheese, grated	3 tbsp
Garlic (*lasan*) paste	2 tsp	Cream, fresh	1/4 cup
Ginger (*adrak*) paste	1 tsp	Garlic paste	1 tsp
Yellow chilli powder	1/2 tsp	Ginger paste	1 tsp
Salt to taste		Dry mango powder (*amchur*)	1/2 tsp
Step II:		Black rock salt (*kaala namak*)	a pinch
Mint (*pudina*) leaves, fresh, blended with		Green cardamom (*choti elaichi*)	
water to make a fine paste	3 tbsp	powder	a pinch
*Hung yoghurt (*dahi*)	1 cup	Cooking oil for basting	1 tbsp

Method

Mix the step I ingredients together in a bowl and rub well into the fish fillets. Keep aside for 15 minutes. Transfer to a strainer to drain excess marinade.

Mix the step II ingredients (except oil) in a bowl. Evenly rub the fish fillets with this marinade and reserve for 45 minutes.

Skewer the fish and roast on a charcoal grill for 5-6 minutes, basting with oil.

Alternatively, the fish can also be roasted in the oven for 7-8 minutes at 120°C / 250°F, turning over once and basting with oil.

Transfer on to a platter and serve.

***Note:** Tie yoghurt in a muslin cloth and hang overnight. The end product after the water has been reduced is called hung yoghurt.*

Chargrilled Pineapple & Sweet Potato Salad

Bhunee Ananaas aur Shakarkandi

Step I:

Pineapple (*ananaas*), medium-sized, peeled, cut into 2" cubes	1
Sweet potatoes, large, washed	1
Star fruit, washed, cut into ¹/₂"-thick roundels	2

Step II:

Balsamic vinegar (*sirka*)	³/₄ cup
Cooking oil	2 tbsp
Sugar, powdered	2 tbsp
Pomegranate (*anaar*) powder	1 tbsp
Kashmiri red chilli powder	1¹/₂ tsp
Cumin (*jeera*) powder	2 tsp
Black rock salt (*kaala namak*), optional	¹/₂ tsp
Black pepper (*kaali mirch*), freshly ground	1 tsp
Dry mango powder (*amchur*)	¹/₂ tsp
Salt to taste	

Method

Boil the sweet potatoes until almost cooked. Peel and cut into ¹/₂"-thick roundels. Keep aside with the rest of the step I ingredients.

Mix the step II ingredients with the palm of your hand on a flat mixing tray. Alternatively, they can also be mixed in a blender.

Add the step I mixture, mix and reserve for 30 minutes.

Preheat oven to 180°C / 350°F. Bake on a roasting tray for 3-4 minutes. Alternatively, the fruit and vegetables can also be skewered and grilled on a charcoal grill.

Transfer on to a platter and serve hot.

Preparation and Cooking time: 45 min. Serves: 4

Spicy Dry Chickpeas
Chana Rawalpindiwaala

Preparation and Cooking Time: 2 hrs. 25 min. Serves: 4

Chickpeas (*kabooli chana*), soaked overnight	450 gm / 1 lb	Pomegranate (*anaar*) powder	5 tsp
Water	12 cups	Dry mango powder (*amchur*)	2 tsp
Soda bi-carbonate	½ tsp	Red chilli powder	1 tsp
Tea bags, tied in a muslin cloth	6	Black rock salt (*kaala namak*)	1 tsp
Step 1:		Dry fenugreek (*kasoori methi*) leaves	2 tsp
Cooking oil	5 tbsp	Cumin (*jeera*) powder	1 tsp
Garlic (*lasan*) paste	2 tsp	Salt to taste	
Gram flour (*besan*)	1 tbsp	Lemon (*nimbu*) juice	1 tbsp
		Ginger (*adrak*), 1" piece, cut into juliennes	1

Method

Boil the chickpeas in water with soda bi-carbonate and tea bags till chickpeas are fully cooked. Drain the water and discard the tea bags.

Heat the oil (step 1) in a wok on medium heat; add garlic paste and sauté until golden brown. Add gram flour and stir and roast for 5-7 minutes ensuring that it does not stick and burn.

Add the remaining ingredients (except ginger); stir for a minute. Add the boiled chickpeas and stir until well mixed. Remove and adjust the seasoning.

Transfer to a serving dish and serve garnished with ginger.

Pickled Aubergines

Achaari Baingan

Aubergines (*baingan*), small and oblong	12	Fennel (*moti saunf*) powder	1 tbsp	
Mustard (*sarson*) oil	1/2 cup	Yellow mustard seed powder	1 1/2 tsp	
Cloves (*laung*)	4	Onion seeds (*kalonji*)	1 1/2 tsp	
Bay leaves (*tej patta*)	2	Coriander (*dhaniya*) powder	1 tbsp	
Asafoetida (*hing*), soaked in 1 tbsp water	a pinch	Carom (*ajwain*) seeds	1/2 tsp	
Step 1:		Red chilli powder	2 tbsp	
Cumin (*jeera*) powder	1 tbsp	Turmeric (*haldi*) powder	1/2 tsp	
Fenugreek seed (*methi dana*)		Dry mango powder (*amchur*)	2 tbsp	
powder	1 1/2 tsp	Salt to taste		

Method

Wash the aubergines in running water, pat dry, slice off the crown, slit crosswise along the length, and keep aside.

Heat the mustard oil in a wok on high heat until it starts smoking. Remove and cool.

Mix the step 1 ingredients together in a bowl.

Pack the aubergines with equal quantities of the above mixture.

Reheat the mustard oil; add cloves, bay leaves, asafoetida, and stuffed aubergines, cover with a lid, and cook on low heat for 12-15 minutes, stirring occasionally. Adjust the seasoning and remove.

Transfer to a flat dish and serve.

Preparation and Cooking time: 50 min. Serves: 4

Stir-fried Corn & Asparagus

Makkai Asparagus Khazaana

Preparation and Cooking time: 1 hr. Serves: 4

Baby corn (*bhutta*)	20	**Step II:**	
Asparagus tips	16	Coriander (*dhaniya*) seeds,	
Step I:		freshly pounded	1 tsp
Cooking oil	¹/₂ cup	Black pepper (*kaali mirch*),	
Cumin (*jeera*) seeds	1 tsp	coarsely ground	1 tsp
Garlic (*lasan*) cloves, peeled,		Cumin powder, roasted	¹/₂ tsp
finely chopped	12	Dry fenugreek leaf (*kasoori methi*)	
Onion, medium-sized, finely chopped	1	powder	¹/₂ tsp
Ginger (*adrak*), 1″ piece, finely chopped	1	Clove (*laung*) powder	a pinch
Green chillies, deseeded,		Cinnamon (*dalchini*) powder	a pinch
finely chopped	2	Lemon (*nimbu*) juice	1 tsp
Tomato purée	¹/₂ cup	Green coriander (*hara dhaniya*),	
Salt to taste		finely chopped	1 tbsp

Method

Heat the oil (step I) in a wok on medium heat; add cumin seeds and sauté till the seeds start spluttering.

Add garlic and sauté until golden brown. Add onion and continue to sauté until light golden brown. Add ginger and green chillies; stir for a minute.

Add corn, stir for a minute. Add the step II ingredients except lemon juice and green coriander. Stir until the spices mix well.

Add tomato purée and continue to stir and roast until specks of oil start to appear. Add asparagus and stir for a minute or until the asparagus is fully cooked.

Add lemon juice and green coriander; stir, remove from heat and serve.

Fish in Coconut Milk with Curry Leaves

Meen Curry

Sole, boneless, cut into 2″ cubes	450 gm / 1 lb

Step I:

Garlic (*lasan*) paste	1³/₄ tsp
Ginger (*adrak*) paste	1¹/₄ tsp
Lemon (*nimbu*) juice	1 tbsp
White pepper (*safed mirch*)	1 tsp
Salt to taste	

Step II:

Coconut (*nariyal*) oil	4 tbsp
Garlic cloves, finely chopped	10
Dry red chillies (*sookhi lal mirch*)	2

Black mustard seeds (*rai*)	1 tsp
Curry leaves (*kari patta*)	16
Green chillies, finely chopped	2
Ginger, finely chopped	1 tsp
Onions, medium-sized, thinly sliced	2
Turmeric (*haldi*) powder	1 tsp
Tomatoes, thinly sliced	2
Salt to taste	
Coconut milk powder, mixed well with 1 cup hot water	1 cup
or Fresh coconut milk (see p. 13)	1 cup

Preparation and Cooking time: 50 min. Serves: 4

Method

Mix the step I ingredients and rub the paste gently over the fish cubes. Keep aside for 30 minutes.

Heat the coconut oil (step II) in a pan on medium heat; add garlic and sauté until it starts changing colour. Add dry red chillies, mustard seeds, and curry leaves; stir.

Add green chillies and ginger; stir well. Add onions and sauté for a minute or until the onions start becoming glossy. Add turmeric powder followed by 1-2 tbsp water and sauté for a minute.

Add fish, tomatoes, and salt; gently stir and roast for a minute taking care not to break the fish.

Add coconut milk, increase heat and bring to the boil. Reduce heat and simmer stirring gently for 1-2 minutes or until fish is fully cooked. Care should be taken not to overcook the fish.

Transfer to a bowl and serve garnished with fried curry leaves.

Crabs Fried with Green Chillies

Kekra Masaleydaar

Crabs (*kekra*), whole	12	Ginger (*adrak*), 1″ piece, cut into juliennes	1
Step 1:		Tomatoes, finely chopped	2
Cooking oil	6 tbsp	Salt to taste	
Garlic (*lasan*), finely chopped	2 tbsp	Coriander (*dhaniya*) powder	1 1/2 tsp
Mustard seeds (*rai*)	1/2 tsp	Turmeric (*haldi*) powder	1/2 tsp
Curry leaves (*kari patta*)	12	Red chilli powder	2 tsp
Onions, medium-sized, thinly sliced	2	Lemon (*nimbu*) juice	1 tbsp
Green chillies, cut into juliennes	2	Cream	1 tbsp

Method

Heat the oil (step 1) till medium hot in a wok; add garlic and sauté till golden brown. Add mustard seeds and curry leaves and sauté until they start spluttering. Add onions and sauté till golden brown.

Add green chillies, ginger, tomatoes, crab, and salt; stir-fry for 1 minute. Add coriander, turmeric and red chilli powders (dissolved in 1/2 cup of water); mix well.

Cook until the liquid evaporates. Add lemon juice and cream and stir until the crab is fully cooked. Remove and adjust the seasoning.

Transfer to a serving dish and serve with bread of your choice.

Chicken with Tomatoes & Mustard Seeds

Rai Tamaterwaala Kararra Murgh

Chicken thighs, boneless,		Onions, medium-sized, thinly sliced	2
cut into 2" cubes	450 gm / 1 lb	Tomatoes, medium-sized, finely chopped	3
Soya sauce	2 tsp	Salt to taste	
Salt to taste		Water	2 cups
Step 1:		Green coriander (*hara dhaniya*),	
Dry red chillies (*sookhi lal mirch*)	10	finely chopped	1 tsp
Mustard seeds (*rai*)	4 tsp	Onion, medium-sized, cut into rings	1
Cooking oil	1/2 cup		

Preparation and Cooking time: 45 min. Serves: 4

Method

Wash the chicken well, shake dry and keep in a strainer to drain excess water.

Mix the soya sauce and salt with the chicken and keep aside for 15-20 minutes.

Grind the dry red chillies (step 1) and mustard seeds together and make a fine powder. Remove to a bowl.

Heat the oil in a pan on high heat; add onions and sauté until light golden brown. Remove to a strainer to drain excess oil.

Reduce heat, and shallow fry the chicken until light golden brown. Remove to a strainer to drain excess oil.

Heat 2 tbsp oil in a pan; add the ground mustard and red chilli mixture, stir for a minute, add tomatoes and continue to stir and roast for 5-6 minutes or until the consistency of the tomatoes resemble a thick sauce. Add water and cook for 5 minutes.

Add the fried onions, chicken, and salt; stir and roast for a minute on high heat. Remove.

Transfer to a serving bowl and serve hot garnished with green coriander and onion rings.

Chicken with Rose Petal Powder

Gulaabi Murgh Pasandey

Chicken breasts, whole, boneless	4 / 600 gm / 22 oz

Step I:

Garlic (*lasan*) paste	1 tbsp
Ginger (*adrak*) paste	1 tbsp
Lemon (*nimbu*) juice	2 tsp
Salt to taste	
Red chilli powder	1 tsp
Black pepper (*kaali mirch*) powder	1 tsp

Step II:

Cooking oil	¹/₂ cup
Onion, medium-sized, thinly sliced	1
Yoghurt (*dahi*)	3 tbsp
Cashew nuts (*kaju*), roasted	12
Gram flour (*besan*), roasted	1¹/₂ tbsp
Rose petal (*gulaab pankhri*) powder	1¹/₂ tsp
Green cardamom (*choti elaichi*) powder	1 tsp

Method

Wash the chicken, shake dry, slice the breast into half horizontally across. It should resemble the shape of a heart and each piece should be ¹/₂" thick.

Mix the chicken with the step I ingredients. Reserve in a strainer for 30 minutes to drain excess water.

Heat the oil (step II) in a pan on high heat; add the onion and sauté until light golden brown. Remove the onions to a strainer to drain excess oil.

Blend the fried onion, yoghurt, and cashew nuts to a fine paste in a blender. Add a little water, if necessary.

On a flat mixing tray, mix the paste with the remaining ingredients of step II. Add the marinated chicken. Mix well and keep aside for 1 hour.

Preheat oven to 180°C / 350°F. Lightly grease a baking tray and lay the marinated chicken slices flat. Bake the chicken for 8-10 minutes, turning it over on its side once in between. Alternatively, the chicken can also be grilled on a charcoal grill.

Transfer on to a platter and serve.

Cinnamon Chargrilled Chicken

Amritsari Bhunna Murgh

Preparation and Cooking time: 1¹/₂ hrs. Serves: 4

Chicken thighs	450 gm / 1 lb	Cumin (*jeera*) powder	1 tsp
Step I:		Black pepper (*kaali mirch*) powder	1 tsp
Malt vinegar (*sirka*)	2 tbsp	Black cardamom (*badi elaichi*) powder	¹/₂ tsp
Ginger (*adrak*) paste	1 tbsp	Cinnamon (*dalchini*) powder	¹/₂ tsp
Garlic (*lasan*) paste	1¹/₂ tbsp	Dry fenugreek leaf (*kasoori methi*)	
Red chilli powder	2 tsp	powder	¹/₂ tsp
Cooking oil	1 tbsp	Kashmiri red chilli powder	¹/₂ tsp
Salt to taste		Cooking oil	2 tbsp
Step II:		Salt to taste	
*Hung yoghurt (*dahi*)	75 gm / 2¹/₂ oz	Lemon (*nimbu*) juice	1 tsp
Pomegranate (*anaar*) powder	2 tsp		

Method

Wash the chicken well, shake dry and keep aside in a strainer to drain excess water.

Mix the step I ingredients in a mixing bowl. Add the chicken, mix well and keep aside for a minimum of 1 hour.

Mix the step II ingredients on a mixing tray. Add the chicken with the marinade in the same tray. Mix well and keep aside for 30 minutes.

Preheat oven to 180°C / 350°F. Bake on a roasting tray for 10-15 minutes or until the chicken is fully cooked. Alternatively, the chicken can also be skewered and grilled on a charcoal grill.

Transfer the chicken on to a platter, drizzle lemon juice and serve.

***Note:** Tie the yoghurt in a muslin cloth and hang overnight. The end product after the water has been reduced is called hung yoghurt.*

Zucchini & Fenugreek Rice

Torai Methi Pulao

Zucchini (*torai*), washed, peeled, halved lengthwise, cut into thin slices	1.350 kg / 3 lb	Ghee	8 tbsp
		Cumin (*jeera*) seeds	2 tsp
Basmati rice, washed few times, soaked for 45 minutes, drained	225 gm / 1/2 lb	Asafoetida (*hing*), dissolved in a little water	2 pinches
		Green chillies, medium-sized, finely chopped	2
Fenugreek (*methi*) leaves, fresh, chopped	120 gm / 4 oz	Ginger (*adrak*), 1" piece, cut into juliennes	1
		Salt to taste	

Method

Sprinkle and rub salt on the fenugreek leaves. Keep aside for 5 minutes and then wash in running water until all traces of salt have been removed. (This is done to reduce the bitterness of the fenugreek). Shake dry and keep aside.

Heat the ghee in a pot; add cumin seeds and asafoetida. When the seeds start to splutter, add the fenugreek leaves. Increase heat to medium and continue to stir and roast for approximately 4-5 minutes or until the oil appears on the sides.

Add zucchini and stir for a minute. Add green chillies and ginger. Add the rice and salt; stir gently. Cover the pot and cook on low heat, stirring gently and occasionally for 10-12 minutes or until the rice is fully cooked and moisture is absorbed.

Transfer to a bowl and serve.

Leavened Wheat Bread with Poppy Seeds
Roti Khus Khaas

Wheat flour (*atta*)	1 3/4 cups	Water	1/2 cup	
Salt to taste		Poppy seeds (*khus khus*)	2 tbsp	
Yeast	1 tsp	Ghee	1 tbsp	
Milk	1 cup			

Preparation and Cooking time: 1 hr. Serves: 4

Method

Soak the yeast in 1/4 cup lukewarm water and reserve for 1 hour in a warm place.

Mix salt and wheat flour together and pass through a sieve to make sure both are mixed well.

Add the yeast mixture and milk to the flour mixture and knead to make a soft and smooth dough. Add water, if necessary. Reserve for 30 minutes.

Divide the dough into 8 portions and shape into balls. Spread some dry refined flour and poppy seeds on a tabletop. Roll the balls over the refined flour so that they are well coated. Dab the poppy seeds with the ball so that one side of the ball is covered with the seeds.

Press the ball with your hand to increase the diameter to 6-8". Repeat with the remaining balls.

Preheat a charcoal fired clay oven (tandoor) to 220°C / 425°F. Place the flattened bread with the poppy seeds side facing down on a small round cushion. Slap the bread on the side of the oven using the cushion and bake until light golden brown. Remove from oven, using tongs or a skewer. The breads can also be baked in a gas tandoor or in a normal oven on a baking tray at the same temperature for 4-5 minutes.

Transfer the breads on to a platter, brush with ghee and serve hot.

Tandoori Bread with Onion Seeds

Naan Kalonji

Refined flour (*maida*)	2¼ cups		Water	1 cup
Baking powder	½ tsp		Cooking oil	2 tbsp
Salt to taste			Black onion seeds (*kalonji*)	2 tsp
Milk	2 cups		Ghee	2 tbsp
Castor sugar	2 tsp			

Method

Mix refined flour, baking powder, and salt in a bowl. Keep aside.

Mix the sugar with the milk. Slowly add the milk to the flour and knead until the dough is soft and smooth.

Once the dough is ready, spread oil over it, punch holes with your finger in random spots and cover with a damp cloth. Keep aside and reserve for 1-2 hours in a warm place.

Divide the dough equally into 8 portions and shape the portions into balls. Spread some dry flour and black onion seeds on a tabletop. Roll the balls over the refined flour so that they are well coated. Dab the onion seeds with the ball so that one side of the ball is covered with the seeds.

Press the ball with your hand to increase the diameter to 6-8". Repeat with the remaining balls.

Preheat a charcoal fired clay oven (tandoor) to 220°C / 425°F. Place the flattened bread with the onion seeds side facing down on a small, round cushion. Slap the bread on the side of the oven using the cushion and bake until light golden brown. Remove from oven, using tongs or a skewer. The breads can also be baked in a gas tandoor or in a normal oven on a baking tray at the same temperature for 3-4 minutes.

Transfer the breads on to a platter, brush with ghee and serve hot.

Stuffed Baked Bread

Bharwaan Amritsari Kulcha

Preparation and Cooking time: 40 min. Serves: 4

Refined flour (*maida*)	450 gm / 1 lb	Green chillies, medium-sized, deseeded, finely chopped	2
Castor sugar	1 tsp	Green coriander (*hara dhaniya*), finely chopped	1 tbsp
Baking powder	a pinch	Black pepper (*kaali mirch*), freshly ground	1 tsp
Salt to taste		Coriander (*dhaniya*) seeds, roasted, freshly pounded	1 tsp
Milk	1 cup	Pomegranate (*anaar*) powder	1 tbsp
Water	1/2 cup	Carom (*ajwain*) seeds	1/2 tsp
Ghee	2 tbsp	Cumin (*jeera*) seeds, roasted	1 tsp
Step 1:		Dry fenugreek (*kasoori methi*) leaves	1 tsp
Potatoes, medium-sized, boiled, peeled, mashed	2	Chilli flakes, roasted	1 tsp
Cauliflower (*phool gobhi*), medium-sized, florets separated and finely grated	1	Salt to taste	
Cottage cheese (*paneer*), grated	50 gm / 1³/₄ oz		
Onion, medium-sized, finely chopped	1	Ghee for brushing	1 tbsp
Ginger (*adrak*), 1″ piece, finely chopped	1		

Method

Mix the first 4 ingredients and pass through a sieve to make sure they are mixed well. Add milk and make a soft and smooth dough. Add more water, if necessary. Add ghee and knead some more. Reserve for 1 hour in a warm place.

Mix the step 1 ingredients to make the stuffing. Check the seasoning and divide into 8-10 portions. Keep aside.

Divide the dough into 8-10 portions and shape each into balls. Spread some refined flour on a tabletop. Roll the balls over the refined flour so that they are well coated. Now make a cup out of each dough ball, fill in the stuffing, and close it on the edges, sealing it completely. Roll it back into ball shape. Press the ball with your hand to increase the diameter to 6-8″. Repeat with the remaining balls.

Preheat a charcoal fired clay oven (tandoor) to 220°C / 425°F. Place the flattened bread on a small round cushion. Slap the bread on the side of the oven using the cushion and bake until light golden brown. Remove, using tongs or a skewer. The breads can also be baked in a gas tandoor or inside a normal oven on a baking tray at the same temperature for 4-5 minutes. Transfer the breads on to a platter, brush with ghee and serve hot.

Carom Layered Bread

Ajwaini Laccha Paratha

Refined flour (*maida*)	3¹/₄ cups	Water	2 cups	
Baking powder	1 tsp	Ghee	5¹/₂ tbsp	
Salt to taste		Cooking oil	3 tbsp	
Carom (*ajwain*) seeds	2 tsp	Red chilli powder	1 tsp	

Method

Mix the refined flour, baking powder, salt, and half the carom seeds together. Add water and knead to a medium soft dough. Reserve for 30 minutes.

Add ghee and knead again until the dough is soft and elastic. Keep aside for 30 minutes.

Divide the dough into 8-10 portions and shape each into balls. Spread some refined flour, red chilli powder, and the remaining carom seeds on a tabletop. Roll the balls over the refined flour so that they are well coated.

Roll the ball with your hands on the table and make a long cylindrical shape. Dab a little ghee over the dough. Take one end and roll it in a spiral to make it back into a round ball.

Press the ball with your hand to increase the diameter to 6-8". Repeat with the remaining dough.

Preheat a charcoal fired clay oven (tandoor) to 220°C / 425°F. Place the flattened bread on a small round cushion. Slap the bread on the side of the oven using the cushion and bake until light golden brown. Remove from oven, using tongs or a skewer. The breads can also be baked in a gas tandoor or in a normal oven on a baking tray at the same temperature for 4-5 minutes.

Transfer the breads on to a platter, brush with ghee and serve hot.

Preparation and Cooking time: 45 min. Serves: 4

109

Rose Petal and Rice Pudding
Gulaab Pankhri ki Kheer

Basmati rice, washed in running water and soaked for 2 hours	½ cup	Milk	4 cups
		Rose petals (*gulaab pankhri*), fresh	12
		Sugar	10 tbsp

Method

Bring the milk to the boil in a pot on medium heat. Add the rose petals and stir.

Add the drained rice to the milk. Reduce heat to low and continue to simmer for 20-25 minutes or until rice is fully cooked.

Add sugar, continue to simmer for 5-7 minutes or until mixture thickens.

Transfer to a serving dish, cool and serve.

Preparation and Cooking time: 45 min. Serves: 4

Almonds: Badaam
Faint, nutty fragrance
and taste

Dates: Khajoor
Rich mahagony colour,
very sweet and creamy

Cashew nuts: Kaju
Rich, sweet nuts with toxic
shell, so they are almost
always sold shelled

Pistachios: Pista

Sold roasted and salted in
their shells; rich in minerals,
vitamins and dietary fibre

Dried Plums: Aloobhukara

Sweet and rich in dietary fibre,
iron, and other nutrients

Raisins: Kishmish

Dried grapes with high
nourishing qualities

dried fruits

Skewered Vegetable Kebabs

Subz Seekh Kebab

Preparation and Cooking time: 1 hr. 25 min. Serves: 4

Dried figs (*anjeer*), finely chopped	2 tbsp	Cheese, mashed		2 tbsp
Almonds (*badaam*), finely chopped	3 tsp	Wholemilk fudge (*khoya*), mashed	30 gm / 1 oz	
Ghee	1 tbsp	Ginger (*adrak*), 1" piece,		
Cumin (*jeera*) seeds	1/2 tsp	finely chopped		1 tsp
French beans, stringed, finely chopped	24	Green chillies, finely chopped		2
Carrots (*gajar*), medium-sized,		Green coriander (*hara dhaniya*),		
finely chopped	2	finely chopped		1 tsp
Salt to taste		Gram flour (*besan*), roasted		1 tbsp
Black pepper (*kaali mirch*) powder	1/2 tsp	Salt to taste		
Potato, medium-sized, washed,		Black peppercorns, crushed		1/2 tsp
boiled, peeled, mashed	1	Cooking butter		1 tsp

Method

Heat the ghee in a pan on medium heat; add cumin seeds and stir for a minute.

Add beans and carrots; stir and roast for 4-5 minutes. Add salt and black pepper, stir for a minute. Remove from heat and cool.

Mix potato, cheese, wholemilk fudge, ginger, green chillies, green coriander, figs, almonds, and gram flour together. Add the bean mixture. Add salt and crushed black pepper; mix well.

Divide the mixture equally into 8 portions. Skewer each portion on a metal skewer with wet hand and shape into 5"-long kebabs.

Put the skewers in the charcoal fired clay oven or grill and cook until kebab is light golden brown.

Remove the skewers and gently pull the kebabs off the skewer by wrapping your palm around the kebab.

Dab gently with cooking butter and arrange on a serving platter.

Green Pea Cakes
Mutterwaali Tikki

Preparation and Cooking time: 45 min. Serves: 4

Green peas (*hara mutter*), frozen	450 gm / 1 lb	Turmeric (*haldi*) powder	1/2 tsp
Step I:		Salt to taste	
Ghee	3 1/4 tbsp	Lemon (*nimbu*) juice	1 tsp
Cumin (*jeera*) seeds	1 tsp	**Step II:**	
Asafoetida (*hing*), dissolved in		Green coriander (*hara dhaniya*),	
a little water	a pinch	finely chopped	1 tbsp
Green chillies, medium-sized,		Gram flour (*besan*), roasted	2 tbsp
deseeded, finely chopped	2	Salted pistachios (*pista*)	12
Ginger (*adrak*), 1" piece, finely chopped	1	Dates (*khajoor*), deseeded,	
Coriander (*dhaniya*) powder	1 tsp	finely chopped	4
Cumin powder	1 tsp	Ghee	4 tbsp

Method

Heat the ghee (step I) in a wok on medium heat; add cumin seeds and stir until the seeds start to splutter. Add asafoetida and stir. Add green chillies and ginger, stir for a minute.

Add green peas, stir for a minute. Add coriander, cumin, and turmeric powders; stir. Add salt, continue to stir and roast for 4-5 minutes or until fully cooked. Add a little water, if necessary. Add lemon juice, stir for a minute. Remove from heat and keep aside to cool.

Transfer the pea mixture to a blender and blend for 2-3 short spurts, until the mixture looks coarsely chopped or like a mince. Take care not to blend the mixture too fine.

Remove to a bowl, add the step II ingredients (except ghee) and mix well.

Divide the mixture into 8 equal portions and shape each portion into 1"-thick flat cake. Place the cakes on a flat tray and keep aside.

Heat the ghee to medium in a pan; fry the cakes until light golden brown on both sides.

Transfer on to a platter and serve hot.

Lamb Balls Stuffed with Dried Plums
Aloobhukara Kofti Kebab

Preparation and Cooking time: 1 hr. 45 min. Serves: 4

Step I:

Lamb leg mince (without fat)	450 gm / 1 lb
Cheddar cheese	90 gm / 3 oz
Green chillies, finely chopped	2
Green coriander (*hara dhaniya*), finely chopped	2¹/₂ tbsp
Garlic (*lasan*) cloves, peeled	12
Ginger (*adrak*), coarsely chopped	2¹/₂ tsp
Onion, medium-sized, finely chopped	1
Black cumin (*shahi jeera*) seeds	¹/₂ tsp
Butter	60 gm / 2 oz
Egg white	1
Gram flour (*besan*), roasted	2 tbsp
Green cardamom (*choti elaichi*) powder	1 tsp
Mace (*javitri*) powder	¹/₂ tsp
Rose petal (*gulaab pankhri*) powder	¹/₂ tsp
Black pepper (*kaali mirch*) powder	¹/₂ tsp
Clove (*laung*) powder	a pinch
Vetivier (*kewra*) water	1 tsp
Salt to taste	

Step II:

Dried plums (*aloobhukara*), finely chopped	12
Green chillies, finely chopped	2
Pistachios (*pista*), peeled, salted, finely chopped	16
Spring onion with stem (*hara pyaz*), large, finely chopped	1
Green coriander, finely chopped	2¹/₂ tbsp
Salt to taste	
Butter	¹/₄ cup
Onions, medium-sized, sliced into thin rings	2

Method

Blend the step I ingredients together in a blender / mincer to a very fine paste. Transfer to a bowl and refrigerate for 30 minutes.

Mix the step II ingredients in a bowl. Keep the filling aside.

Take the cooled mince and divide equally into 16 portions. With wet hands, take a portion, flatten with your hand, put a bit of filling in the centre and make it into a smooth round ball. Care should be taken to see that the balls are tightly packed.

Preheat oven to 180°C / 350°F. Transfer the balls to a lightly oiled baking tray and bake for 15 minutes. Remove from oven, baste with butter and bake for another 15-20 minutes or until balls are fully cooked.

Transfer to a flat dish and serve garnished with onion rings and accompanied with mint chutney (see p. 13).

Crispy Bitter Gourd

Amchur ke Karelay

Step I:

Bitter gourd (*karela*), medium-sized, washed, scraped, slit lengthwise, seeds discarded, thinly sliced	6
Turmeric (*haldi*) powder	I tsp
Red chilli powder	I tsp
Salt to taste	
Malt vinegar (*sirka*)	2 tbsp

Step II:

Mustard (*sarson*) oil	2 cups
Onions, medium-sized, thinly sliced	4

Carom (*ajwain*) seeds	$^{1}/_{2}$ tsp
Ginger (*adrak*)	I tsp
Asafoetida (*hing*), mixed in a little water	a pinch
Dry mango powder (*amchur*)	I tsp
Cumin (*jeera*) powder	I tsp
Black pepper (*kaali mirch*) powder	$^{1}/_{2}$ tsp
Red chilli powder	I tsp
Fennel (*moti saunf*) powder	$^{1}/_{2}$ tsp
Dry fenugreek (*kasoori methi*) leaf powder	$^{1}/_{2}$ tsp
Lemon (*nimbu*) juice	I tsp

Preparation and Cooking time: 50 min. Serves: 4

Method

Mix the step I ingredients with the bitter gourd. Rub with your hands to ensure that the gourd gets well coated with the spices. Keep aside for 30 minutes, then wash in running water and shake dry. Keep aside.

Heat the mustard oil (step II) in a wok on high heat until it starts smoking. Reduce heat until smoking stops and oil reaches medium temperature. Fry the onions in the oil until golden brown, remove to a strainer to drain excess oil. Fry the bitter gourd in the same oil on medium high heat until crisp and golden brown. Remove and drain the excess oil.

Heat 2 tbsp mustard oil on medium heat; add carom seeds, ginger, and asafoetida; stir well.

Increase heat to high, add the bitter gourd and stir for a minute. Sprinkle mango, cumin, black pepper, red chilli, fennel and fenugreek powders. Stir to mix well. Mix in the fried onions and adjust the seasoning. Add lemon juice, stir and remove from heat.

Transfer to a bowl and serve.

Vegetable Qorma
Navrattan Subz Qorma

Carrots (*gajar*), diced into 1" pieces	50 gm / 1³/₄ oz
French beans, diced	50 gm / 1³/₄ oz
Cottage cheese (*paneer*), diced into 1" pieces	100 gm / 3¹/₂ oz
Cashew nuts (*kaju*), roasted	12
Green peas (*hara mutter*), fresh or frozen	80 gm / 2³/₄ oz

Step I:

Ginger (*adrak*)	1³/₄ tsp
Garlic (*lasan*)	1³/₄ tsp
Onion	80 gm / 2³/₄ oz
Wholemilk fudge (*khoya*)	20 gm
Yoghurt (*dahi*)	¹/₂ cup
Green chillies, deseeded	2

Step II:

Ghee	5 tbsp
Green cardamom (*choti elaichi*)	2
Cinnamon (*dalchini*), 1" sticks	2
Salt to taste	
Water	1 cup
Green cardamom powder	³/₄ tsp
White pepper (*safed mirch*)	2 tsp
Aniseed (*saunf*) powder	1³/₄ tsp
Cherries, fresh, deseeded, halved	6
Pineapple (*ananaas*), fresh, cut into 1" cubes	2
Strawberries, fresh, cut into quarters	4
Green grapes (*angoor*)	12
Lemon (*nimbu*) juice	1 tbsp
Cream	¹/₂ cup

Method

Mix the step I ingredients together and blend to a fine paste.

Heat 3¹/₂ tbsp ghee (step II) in a pot and set to medium heat; add green cardamom and cinnamon sticks; stir until the cardamom changes colour. Add the blended paste and stir and roast until fat appears on the sides. Add salt and water (or vegetable stock, see p. 13). Increase heat to high and bring the mixture to the boil. Reduce heat and simmer for 2-3 minutes. Remove from heat.

Strain the mixture through a soup strainer. Keep the liquid and discard the pulp.

Clean the pot and heat the remaining ghee to medium hot. Add carrots, beans, cottage cheese, cashew nuts, and green peas; sauté for a minute. Add the green cardamom, white pepper, and aniseed powders; mix. Add the strained liquid. Bring to the boil, add all the fruits and stir. Add lemon juice; stir well. Stir in the cream. Bring to the boil, adjust the seasoning and remove from heat. Transfer to a bowl and serve.

Andhra Fish Curry

Andhra Macchi Curry

Step I:

Sole, boneless, cut into 2″ cubes	450 gm / 1 lb
Garlic (*lasan*) paste	1 tbsp
Ginger (*adrak*) paste	1 tbsp
Lemon (*nimbu*) juice	1 tbsp
Red chilli powder	2 tbsp
White pepper (*safed mirch*) powder	1 tsp
Salt to taste	

Step II:

Dry red chillies (*sookhi lal mirch*)	6
Cumin (*jeera*) seeds	2 tsp
Desiccated coconut powder (*nariyal burada*)	2 tbsp
Coriander (*dhaniya*) seeds, crushed	1 tbsp
Garlic cloves, roughly chopped	18
Ginger, 1″ piece, roughly chopped	1
Turmeric (*haldi*) powder	1 tsp
Onions, medium-sized, thinly sliced	1

Step III:

Coconut oil	6 tbsp
Black mustard seeds (*rai*)	2 tsp
Curry leaves (*kari patta*)	12
Tomato purée	2 1/2 cups
Tamarind (*imli*), soaked in 1 cup water	60 gm / 2 oz
Coconut milk powder, mixed well with 1 cup hot water	1 cup
or Fresh coconut milk (see p. 13)	1 cup
Salt to taste	

Method

Mix the step I ingredients together and keep aside for 30 minutes.

Mix the step II ingredients in a pan (except garlic, ginger, turmeric powder, and onions). Dry roast the mixture on medium heat for a few minutes or until the ingredients change colour to light brown. Cool, and blend to a fine paste with the remaining ingredients in a blender with little water.

Heat the oil (step III) in a pan on medium heat; add mustard seeds and curry leaves; sauté until a popping sound is heard. Add the paste and continue to stir and roast until fat starts to appear on the sides. Add the tomato purée and stir and roast until fat appears on the sides.

Strain the tamarind, discard the pulp and add the water to the pan. Bring to the boil, add the marinated fish and continue to cook, stirring gently for 3-4 minutes, taking care not to break the fish. Add coconut milk and bring to the boil. Reduce heat and simmer stirring gently for a minute. Check the seasoning and remove from heat.

Transfer to a bowl and serve.

Stuffed Chicken Breasts in Pistachio Sauce

Shahi Murgh Pisteywaala

Step I:

Chicken breasts, whole, boneless	4 / 600 gm / 22 oz
Ginger (*adrak*) paste	1 tbsp
Garlic (*lasan*) paste	1¹/₂ tbsp
Lemon (*nimbu*) juice	1 tbsp
Salt to taste	
White pepper (*safed mirch*) powder	1 tsp

Step II:

Cooking butter	2 tbsp
Ginger, 1″ piece, finely chopped	1
Green chillies, medium-sized, deseeded, finely chopped	3
Onion, medium-sized, finely chopped	1
Chicken breasts, without fat, coarsely minced	200 gm / 7 oz
Salt to taste	
Green cardamom (*choti elaichi*) powder	¹/₂ tsp
Mace (*jaiphal*) powder	a pinch
Black pepper (*kaali mirch*) powder	¹/₂ tsp

Green coriander (*hara dhaniya*), finely chopped	1 tbsp
Unsalted pistachios (*pista*), shelled, finely sliced	18
Raisins (*kishmish*), finely chopped	12
Butter for roasting	1¹/₂ tbsp

Step III:

Ghee	70 gm / 2¹/₄ oz
Ginger paste	1³/₄ tsp
Garlic paste	3¹/₄ tsp
Onions, medium-sized, blended into a paste	2
Coriander (*dhaniya*) powder	2 tsp
Yoghurt (*dahi*)	¹/₂ cup
Unsalted pistachio paste	60 gm / 2 oz
Chicken stock (see p. 13)	1 cup
Salt to taste	
Lemon juice	1 tsp
Mace powder	a pinch
Green cardamom powder	1 tsp
Rose water (*gulaab jal*)	2 drops
Cream, fresh	50 ml / 1³/₄ fl oz

Method

Wash the chicken well, shake dry, slice each breast into half horizontally across. It should resemble the shape of a heart and each piece should be ¹/₂″ thick

Mix the step I ingredients together in a bowl. Reserve in a strainer for 30 minutes to drain excess water.

Heat the cooking butter (step II) in a pan on medium heat; add ginger, green chillies, and onion; sauté for 2-3 minute. Add chicken mince and stir and roast till fat appears in the side. Add salt, stir. Add green cardamom, mace, and black pepper powders; stir. Add green coriander and sauté for a minute. Remove from heat, transfer to a bowl and when it cools add pistachios and raisins; mix well. Divide into 8 equal parts. Keep aside.

Preheat oven to 180°C / 350°F. Take the marinated chicken slices and lay them out flat. Place the chicken mince mixture on top of the slices and roll tightly to form small rolls. Push a toothpick through the roll to keep it in place. Grease the roasting tray with half the butter and place the chicken pieces over it, spreading the remaining butter on top. Cover the tray with silver foil and bake the chicken for 8-10 minutes.

Heat the ghee (step III) in a pan on medium heat; add ginger-garlic pastes; sauté for a minute. Add onion paste and coriander powder; stir and roast until fat starts to appear on the side. Add yoghurt and stir and roast until fat appears again. Add pistachio paste and stir and roast until specks of fat start to appear.

Add chicken stock and salt, increase heat and bring to the boil. Reduce heat to low, stirring occasionally for 2-3 minutes. Add lemon juice, stir, add mace and green cardamom powders, rose water, and cream; stir for a minute, remove from heat and transfer to a bowl.

Place the baked chicken pieces on a serving platter, pour the gravy over the pieces and bake at 180°C / 350°F for 2-3 minutes.

Remove from oven, garnish with finely sliced green pistachios (optional) and serve hot.

Roasted Almond Confection

Badaam ka Halwa

Almonds (*badaam*), roasted, peeled	1¹/₂ cups	Ghee	4 tbsp
Milk	2¹/₂ cups	Green cardamom (*choti elaichi*) seeds	1¹/₂ gm
Sugar	10 tbsp	Saffron (*kesar*)	1 tsp
		Pistachios (*pista*), shelled, sliced	12

Method

Bring the milk to the boil on medium heat. Reduce heat to low and continue to stir and cook until milk reduces to half its original quantity. Add the sugar and continue to stir and cook until the mixture is reduced to half. Remove from heat.

Heat the ghee in a wok on medium heat. Add the almonds and stir and roast until light golden. Add the milk mixture, green cardamom seeds, and saffron and continue to cook until the moisture dries completely.

Transfer to a bowl and serve hot garnished with pistachios.

Preparation and Cooking time: 1 hr. 45 min. Serves: 4

index